you gotta want it

JAKE PAUL

SIMON & SCHUSTER

London · New York · Sydney · Toronto · New Delhi

A CBS COMPANY

you

gotta

want

it

First published in Great Britain by Simon & Schuster UK Ltd, 2016
A CBS COMPANY

NOTE TO READERS:
Some names and identifying characteristics have been changed.

1 3 5 7 9 10 8 6 4 2

Simon & Schuster UK Ltd
1st Floor
222 Gray's Inn Road
London WC1X 8HB

www.simonandschuster.co.uk
www.simonandschuster.com.au
www.simonandschuster.co.in

Simon & Schuster Australia, Sydney
Simon & Schuster India, New Delhi

The author and publishers have made all reasonable efforts to contact copyright-holders for permission, and apologise for any omissions or errors in the form of credits given. Corrections may be made to future printings.

A CIP catalogue record for this book is available from the British Library

Hardback ISBN: 978-1-4711-6151-3
eBook ISBN: 978-1-4711-6152-0

Interior design by Akasha Archer
Printed and bound by CPI Group (UK) Ltd, Croydon, CR0 4YY

Simon & Schuster UK Ltd are committed to sourcing paper that is made from wood grown in sustainable forests and support the Forest Stewardship Council, the leading international forest certification organisation. Our books displaying the FSC logo are printed on FSC certified paper.

Dedicating this book to my fans and supporters,
to my mom and dad, who have helped me get to where I am,
and to the people who want it in life.
And if you don't want it . . .
You Gotta Want It

CONTENTS

CONTENTS   ix

You Gotta Want It

/yo͞o, yə/ ˈgädə/wänt, wônt/it/

pronoun-contraction-verb-pronoun

1. When you pursue a passion, dream, or desire with the single-minded purpose of making it real.

2. The act of being so determined that nothing can stop you.

3. What you tell yourself when the odds are stacked against you but achieving your goal still seems possible—even if you're the only one who believes it.

ME, IN ABOUT 6 SECONDS (MORE OR LESS)

- Hi, my name is Jake Paul. But you probably knew that.
- I make funny videos and post them online. You probably knew that, too.
- I'm nineteen years old.
- I played Lance in YouTube's first-ever film, *Dance Camp*, and I now play Dirk on the Disney Channel series *Bizaardvark*.
- You'll never see me at the club. You'll never see me at the late-night house party. You'll never see me drinking. You'll never see me smoking. I'm all about a strong work ethic and striving to achieve my goals—all while having fun, of course.
- I like being creative, making funny videos, and hanging out with friends—usually all at the same time.
- People always ask what's the most embarrassing thing that's happened to me. My answer? I don't get embarrassed. But I do laugh at myself a lot—that's kind of the point, right?
- I'm into cars and trucks. My dream car is a Pagani Zonda. What's a Zonda? It's super fast, and super cool.
- There's a place around the corner from where I live that has killer smoothies. My favorite is peanut butter and jelly. I got one a few minutes ago.
- I am wearing Yeezy shoes right now. Yup, those are Kanye's.

- My first-ever, waste-your-money splurge? A gold Rolex. I thought it would make me cool in Hollywood. I was wrong.
- Being ourselves makes us cool.
- I'm wearing sweatpants.
- I do not have a girlfriend right now. Do you know anyone?[1]
- By the time you read this, I will have moved into an awesome house. But right now I live in a two-bedroom apartment in Hollywood, with five or six other people, including my brother, Logan. It's like an open house: People come in and out all day and night, and it looks like it. Inside, there's a huge pile of sneakers, a hundred pairs or more. I don't remember how it began, but it's grown into a giant art installation. For furniture, we have a bunch of extra-large beanbag chairs. Twenty people could crash comfortably, and sometimes they do. The kitchen is used—constantly. Cleanup is an issue. I'm staring at a bunch of leftover food on the counter. Don't know what month it's from. So you get the picture, and understand why I will have moved.
- My brother, Logan, is standing next to me. He says this book should be titled *6 Seconds*, and he is telling me it should be all about girls. But I say, "No, this book is all about . . ."
- That's a good question. What is this book about?

---

1 DM me.

SO WHERE TO BEGIN?

When I was in high school I used to dread opening a book. I hated turning to page one. All I thought about was how many more pages I had to read to get to the end and how much time that was going to take. The books were big and the print was small. There weren't many pictures, either. And they weren't funny. (Has anyone ever written a funny textbook? I have written many funny things *inside* textbooks, but that's not the same thing.)

I was impatient. I wanted to know the important stuff right away. I wished there was a way to ingest all that information quickly. I had other stuff to do, like make videos with my brother, Logan.

You get the point. I wasn't much of a reader. I've read maybe three books in my entire life. You may be different. After all, you are looking at this book right now, and hopefully you plan to read the whole thing. If not, if you only want to read the good parts, I wrote a chapter for you. It's titled "Just the Good Parts." Turn there now if you're that person. But in the event you are like me and want to know what this is about before you invest time in reading any further, I'll tell you right now.

The book is about you!

It's about motivating you to live your dream.

To that end, you'll find this book is also about me, and how a normal, average jock, bro-type of guy with a creative and goofy side moved to Hollywood from Ohio and created a successful business from something he loved to do. It's about being a teenager with an idea and turning that idea into a reality, and then working my ass off to grow that reality into something that today seems like a fantasy— except it's not. It's real. And by telling my story, I want to convince you that you can have the same success in whatever you love to do.

I know a lot of kids—and maybe you're one of them—who sit in their bedroom and think, *I'm only fifteen* or *I'm only seventeen years old, and I can't do this or that, it's too hard, I'm too young, it's never going to happen.* I want to tell you to stop thinking that way. In fact, that may be the most important sentence I'm going to write. *Stop thinking that way!*

Whether you want to become Internet famous or create a company, if you want to start a record label or become a doctor, a model in Hollywood, or chase your digital dreams in Silicon Valley, my goal here in this book is to inspire you to go for it. Move with deliberate fearlessness. Defy the odds that are supposedly against success. Ignore the naysayers. Take the word *no*, flip it around, and say to yourself, "I'm *on it*."

Let me tell you a quick story. One night not too long ago, my brother and I decided to drive to Las Vegas. We took his car, a purple Dodge Challenger SRT8. It was two in the morning, and I was behind the wheel. We had the music blasting, the warm air was rushing in, and we were on a completely deserted road. I turned to Logan and said, "Let's see how fast we can go."

"Do it," he said.

I stepped on the gas pedal. The Challenger's massive engine growled. Instantly, Logan and I were pushed back into our seats as the car blasted forward. The speedometer soared past 170. I glanced around. There was no traffic anywhere near us and no cops in sight. I said, "I'm going to gun it like this the whole way." My brother nod-ded. I stared straight ahead. In front of me, for as far as I could see, there was nothing but open road, and I was going for it.

Which is my approach to everything. It should be yours, too.

Anything you can dream of is possible. I know what I'm talking about—because it happened to me. . . .

ZOOSH

If you're in or around my generation and have grown up 100 percent digital, your life is pretty much documented on your phone. Mine is. I have thousands of photos on my 6. I also have exactly 1,900 videos. That's a big, round, intimidating number. But there should be 1,901. I'm missing one particular video, and I'm pissed about it.

It's a video of me jumping off the plane the day I arrived in Los Angeles. Literally. I was seventeen years old, the plane had landed and taxied to the gate, and as I got to the door I whipped out my phone, pressed record, and began narrating the start of my adventure to the tune of a Miley Cyrus song. "I hopped off the plane at LAX with a dream . . ." Then I literally hopped off the plane, timed perfectly to the lyric, and continued to serve up my own commentary.

"And no one's going to stop me from conquering my dream. I don't know what it is I'm going to do, but I'm going to work hard and do it."

In light of all I've achieved since then, that video means a lot to me. It captured the exact moment when I planted my flag and vowed with total seriousness to myself that I would succeed. It was intense. I remember every moment perfectly, which is why I'm so bummed I can't find that video. I can still feel the determination I had as I stepped off that plane. If I were a rapper, I'd be flowing off that day forever. I listen to a lot of rap. I relate to it. I know rappers exaggerate to make their songs more street, but when I decipher the lyrics, they're mostly about stuff that's happened, or is happening, to those guys as they fight their way to the top. Nothing's going to stop 'em, they say—and I know exactly what they mean.

I don't think anything's random. If something's meant to happen, it'll happen. If you're meant for it and want it bad enough, it'll happen. My brother and I got lucky, but we were also prepared to take advantage of the opportunities that came our way—and then kick it to the next level. I didn't realize until much later that we actually started preparing for Internet fame long before either of us moved to Hollywood, and certainly long before my first day in the City of Angels.

As far as I'm concerned, our journey began the day my dad gave my brother and me a little handheld Sony video camera. It was Christmas 2007. I was ten years old, and Logan was twelve. We were stoked. My dad bought the camera to record our football games, so we could replay the games later. We wanted to study the plays and our technique, and learn and grow from our victories—and our mistakes.

Immediately, Logan and I started messing around with the camera. I'm pretty sure we began making videos the day we got it and took it from there. We had fun. We pointed the camera at each other while goofing around. Those earliest videos were of me riding around on our four-wheeler and my brother doing backflips on the trampoline. Logan uploaded the footage on his computer and edited it into short videos. They made us laugh, but that was it. At the time, they were meaningless.

Then we started watching YouTube and discovered a channel called Smosh. At the time, it was the biggest channel on YouTube, and we found this guy whose videos made us laugh. His name was Ryan Higa, but he went by the name Nigahiga. He was a dude from Hawaii, not too much older than us, and into sports and being stupid

funny. He lip-synched. He made fart jokes. It was simple comedy—
setup and punch line—kind of like the videos Logan and I made, except he was putting his videos on YouTube—and tons of people were
watching them.

Before going any further, though, I want to give you more insight
into my family. Logan and I are the only two children of Greg Paul
and Pamela Stepnick. My brother will have to tell you about his ar-
rival into this world, because I don't know the details. As for me, I was
three weeks early. I couldn't wait, which is typical of me. According to
my mom, I was colicky and had a predilection for projectile vomiting,
but otherwise was a good eater and a great sleeper, and as both a baby
and a little kid I always smiled.

In fact, I just called my mom to ask what kind of baby I was. You
know what she said? "Awesome."

Thanks, Mom!

My parents divorced when I was in kindergarten. I was too young
to be affected by their split, and I don't know any of the details. By
the time I was old enough to figure things out, my mom was remarried and my dad was into the ladies, and I didn't feel the need to ask
them questions. My mom was cool, funny, and hands-on—literally,
as she often helped us shoot our videos when we needed someone to
work the camera; and as for my dad, I have to describe him as "the
legend Greg Paul" rather than just "my dad." He's that kind of guy.[2]

Even divorced, my parents were totally cool with each other—and
they still are. Their priority was always clear: being good parents to
Logan and me. We were always well cared for and made to feel loved.

---

2 My dad called me up after reading this and said, "Pretty accurate."

We knew it, and the confidence that gave us no doubt explains our outgoing, positive personalities. I knew I could push the boundaries with my mom and still get a hug at the end of the day. She's saved the cards and letters I've written her over the years for birthdays, Mother's Day, and holidays, and almost all of them begin with me saying a variation of the same thing: "Thanks for putting up with me and taking care of me. I appreciate everything you do."

We lived in Westlake, a suburb about ten miles outside of downtown Cleveland. My parents lived three miles from each other, which made splitting time between the two of them pretty easy. My dad's house was out in the woods with a super-long driveway and outdoor space that Logan and I definitely took advantage of. We rode our four-wheelers, ran sprints down the driveway, and spent all our time outside in the summers when we weren't watching videos or screwing around in front of the camera making our own.

My mom's house was in a more traditional, well-tended neighborhood. She remarried a doctor, and they lived in a modern-style house with a backyard that had enough room for shooting hoops. Logan and I shot a ton of our early videos there, too. If you can't tell by now, the two of us had a great relationship, totally bro-to-bro. I don't have memories of myself as a kid that don't include Logan, and given our interests, most of those memories have something to do with playing or watching sports.

Logan and I were always competitive. He was two years older, so we didn't play against each other in organized leagues—only in the backyard. He was a star athlete in every sport he played, which gave me a target to aim for as I came up the ranks. By the time I was his age, I tried to beat his accomplishments. For example, when he was in sixth grade, he scored twenty-something touchdowns in a single season of football. That's an incredible number; as I said, he was a superstar. But when I was in sixth grade, I knew I had to beat his record, and so I worked to pass his target and scored thirty-something touchdowns.

That friendly but competitive vibe pretty much permeated everything we did, and we loved it. We were each other's biggest fans. I think that's why we worked together so well when we got into making videos. It was easy. We laughed at the same things, and basically tried to make each other laugh even harder than the previous time. And so, once we got our hands on that camera, it was game on. We worked together to be funnier than the guys who were making it on YouTube.

A few months after we got the camera, my brother got a MacBook. It was the computer equivalent to getting a sports car. We'd been working on a clunky desktop computer, but like you, we grew up digital, and we wanted the newest and fastest devices. To us, that MacBook was the best—and it was our YouTube autobahn. I spent hours watching videos. I never really watched TV, at least not the way my parents and almost anyone else older than me did. Like you, I'm from a different generation. I have always chosen what I want to watch. I just type in a bunch of search words and laugh my ass off. It's much more satisfying.

I looked up to the YouTube entertainers who made me laugh. They were a new breed of star. I related to them, and wondered what they were like away from the camera, in real life. The people Logan and I watched on YouTube were eighteen and nineteen years old, older than us but still in their teens. I never thought I could become one of them, but that didn't stop us from creating our videos.

In those earliest days, Logan and I rarely planned out our videos. I picked up the camera, pointed it at my brother, and asked, "Hey, what are you doing?" He said, "Uhhhhhhh," acted totally dumb and spazzy, and we improvised from there. If we cracked ourselves up, we were good. If not, we clicked delete and tried again. We were best at lip-synching pop songs and pranking strangers in public places. Our parents were good sports, too. If we saw my dad working in the garden, we rushed outside with the camera shouting, as if we'd never seen this before, "Hey, Dad's in the garden!" A natural ham, he stood up, flexed his biceps, and said, "Yo, G.P. in the house. Chicks dig me." We dug him, too—and laughed. Something funny always happened.

One day, after about four or five months, Logan was editing a video, as he always did, while I looked over his shoulder, offering opinions, as I always did. We were laughing and talking about the video, trading ideas and ranking the video we were working on against all the other videos we'd made previously. Every new one seemed like the funniest one to us, until we started going through the old ones, and then those seemed funny again. Suddenly Logan, in a moment of inspiration that would change our lives, said, "We should have our own YouTube channel and upload our videos."

It was not an exceptionally unique idea, but what was unique about it was that we actually did it! We acted on it.

"What are we going to name it?" I asked.

"It's gotta be something cool and good," Logan said.

"And catchy."

"Yeah." He nodded.

"It's gotta be something our fans are going to like."

"We don't have any fans," he said.

"Still."

After some time spent thinking and trying out various names, we decided to call it Zoosh. We thought it sounded kind of like Smosh. That's as much meaning as the name had. Zoosh didn't mean anything, but it was ours, and we went with it. We created the channel, uploaded videos, and launched a huge marketing campaign—us telling all of our friends about it, and telling them to tell their friends.

That's what made us take Zoosh seriously—or as seriously as we could. Making these videos was something we did after football practice, homework, dinner, and chores. It was the way we entertained ourselves. From the start, our friends loved our videos, and that was powerful motivation to keep making them. I was now in fifth grade and Logan was in seventh, and every day we heard things like "You guys are so funny" or "Oh my God, that video you guys put up last weekend is insane!" Then our friends got bolder. They asked if they could be in one. "Dude, if you ever need someone." Or they were even more blatant: "Can you put me in your next video?"

The reason our friends wanted to be in them? People were watching them. Zoosh grew beyond our friends and classmates; the circle kept widening until one of our videos got a thousand views, which blew Logan and me away. It was mind-boggling. A thousand views!

Now my videos have combined for several billion views, but back then a thousand views was insane, incomprehensible. Logan and I were just kids. We were having fun in our spare time. Views didn't matter to us back then, and we didn't even check our views regularly. Sometimes we went weeks before remembering to refresh and see if anyone had watched the videos. The reactions we got from our friends were more important than the number of views. But then we made the video that became our first hit. It got more than one thousand views, and I'm not going to lie—hitting that number was really thrilling.

In the video, Logan and I talked through songs as if we were speaking to each other. He lip-synched Taylor Swift lyrics to me and I responded with lyrics from another song. We went back and forth like that and made a story out of it. Like an exaggerated comedic drama. We put it up on YouTube and got a couple of hundred views pretty quickly. Then, all of a sudden, the views jumped to four hundred. Then they went to eight hundred. And then, amazingly, they shot past a thousand!

As we did with all our videos, we showed my parents—separately, of course, since, as you'll recall, they were divorced. After they finished laughing—and they really did laugh—I turned to my brother with a confused look on my face. He was intently watching something on his laptop, so I threw a ball at him to get his attention. He turned around.

"What's up?"

"Mom thought that video was funny, right?"

"She laughed."

"And Dad thought it was funny, too, right?"

"He cracked up."

"Yeah," I said. "But I can't figure out if they were laughing with us—or if they were laughing at us."

My brother pulled up the video on his screen and leaned back so I could see it from where I was sitting. He clicked play and we watched the video. Pretty soon, the two of us were dying of laughter. Whenever we got ourselves laughing, we knew it was genuinely hilarious.

"That's sick," he said.

I agreed.

We were funny.

The video was funny.

It made us laugh.

Nothing else mattered.[3]

---

3 Okay, that was a long story, and it turned into a really long chapter. To those of you who like one- or two- or three-page chapters so you feel like you're making progress, I apologize. I'll make the next chapter short.

A SHORT CHAPTER

WHAT INSPIRES YOU?

PAM STEPNICK (MY MOM): 5 THINGS I KNOW ABOUT JAKE THAT YOU DON'T (INCLUDING THE MYSTERY OF JAKE'S MISSING EYEBROWS)

1. When he was little, he had a favorite blankie. It was white with his last name stitched on it. He carried it every single place he went—day care, back and forth between his dad's house and my house. I still have it.

2. As a little boy, he always wanted to wear basketball shorts to school—even when it was raining or the middle of winter. It was kind of stupid to do that when it was below freezing and snowing outside. When I told him he had to wear long pants, he wore his basketball shorts *over* his pants. He looked hilarious, but he did it every day.

3. He cannot stand anyone touching his belly button. As a result, he'd let his belly button get dirty. At times, there was enough lint in there to knit a sweater. His dad would have to hold him down to clean it out. Jake would be screaming and crying. He hated it. The last time I saw him, I checked to see if it was clean. It was.

4. Oh, and do not touch his toes. But he hates his belly button being touched more.

5. Then there's the mystery of his missing eyebrows. When he was in fourth or fifth grade, Jake decided to shave off half of his eyebrows. He shaved from the middle of the eye out toward the end. He literally shaved them off. To this day, Jake hasn't ever told us why. He pretends like nothing happened, and when we ask him directly, he ignores us. PS—I'd still like to know.

WHY'D YOU DELETE THAT VIDEO?

Even though I was only in sixth grade, I already had a reputation in my school and the local junior high. My brother paved the way. He was a star in everything he did, from academics to sports. Thanks to him, I enjoyed last-name-notoriety from the first day of every school year. "Oh, you're Logan's younger brother."

When I finally got to junior high, I quickly forged my own identity, though not as an academic whiz. As my mom tells it, I was a smart kid who fidgeted in class and vied with the teacher for the class's attention by being funny. In other words, I was a class clown.

I did much better on the football field. I had a cool visor on my helmet and wore awesome socks. I also scored a lot of touchdowns.

And I was known as the costar of videos that periodically made the you-gotta-see-it lists at our respective schools.

I say "periodically" because we produced only two or three videos per month. Today, most social influencers agree the formula for success begins with a steady output of at least one new video each week. You have to feed your audience and keep your fans entertained, and be consistent. But back when I was in sixth grade and my brother was in eighth, we weren't out to entertain anyone else—just ourselves. Our ideas were created on the fly. As we shot the scenes, one of us suggested lines, another chimed in, and the video came together.

There was no holding back, either. I had dozens of cuts, scrapes, and bruises. I bled for those punch lines. I jumped into cars. Logan dove out of windows. We didn't know how to fake anything. I remember shooting several videos where my brother said, "I'm going to slap you in this part." I said, "Okay." Then he wound up and slapped me—and I went flying! The sound of his hand connecting with my face was painfully real. Within seconds, my cheek looked like a splattered tomato.

In another video, I looked up as a football came falling down from the sky and hit me square in the face. We did numerous takes, too. It was so funny on-screen, but so painful in real life. Pain was not the point, though; comedy perfection was.

But not everyone saw the humor in our channel. One time, I had this idea of doing a take on MTV's *True Life* series, specifically the episode titled "I'm a Nerd." As soon as the idea popped into my head, I turned to my brother and said, "Hey, I'm a nerd," in a dull, nasally voice, paired with a dorky face.

"Hi, my name is Barry and I'm a nerd," I said, pronouncing the name "Bear-reee."

The name just popped into my head.

Logan laughed.

"Okay, we're going to follow Bear-reee through his daily life and see what he does," my brother said.

During the shoot, we laughed harder than ever before. We posted the finished work on Zoosh, and it looked like it was going to be our most popular video yet. The views sailed into the hundreds immediately; we predicted they would soar into the thousands eventually. People talked about the video at school. Everyone loved it—except for one person, a guy named Barry. He was the kid many people at school knew and thought of as a nerd.

I'm not going to say whether Barry was a student or someone people knew from sports and neighborhood activities; it doesn't matter. What does matter is that this intersection of our video—and more specifically my caricature of a nerd—and someone's real life was a really, really unfortunate coincidence, one that, in retrospect, was just not cool at all.

I know the evidence suggests otherwise, but to this day I swear I did not have anyone in mind when I blurted out the name Barry. Nor did I have anyone in mind when I played a nerd in front of the camera. I was thinking of the MTV show, and that's it. I swore the same to my dad a few nights after it posted, when he came into my bedroom and said there was a problem with the video.[4] The conversation went something like this:

"I got a call from this kid's father, who said you're making fun of his son—"

"But I'm not," I said.

My dad gave me a stern, this-isn't-a-joke look that would have easily squeezed the truth from me had I been lying, which I wasn't.

"Let me finish," he said. "He said you're making fun of his son. His son's name is Barry. What's your name in the video?"

"Barry," I said.

"How'd you say it in the video?"

"Bear-reee."

I had a hard time not laughing.

"Really, Jake?"

I knew better than to answer.

My dad continued: "His father said they're going to take it to the school's principal if you don't delete the video—"

---

4 He put special emphasis on the word *problem*, so that immediately I knew the gravity of the so-called problem was closer to him wondering when I'd had a lobotomy than it was to, say, having eaten all his Doritos.

"Delete it?" I said, alarmed.

"And go over to his house and apologize to him."

"You can't make me delete it," I protested. "It's the funniest video we've ever made." I have to confess, at that moment, I wasn't thinking of Barry. I was thinking of all the views we'd miss out on.

"Not everyone's laughing."

The video came down, and soon I was sitting in the passenger seat of my dad's Toyota 4Runner, heading to Barry's house to deliver an in-person apology. On the way, my dad made sure I understood the whole situation. Barry's entire family was upset, he said, and no matter what I did or didn't intend, Barry felt bullied and hurt, and so I had to take responsibility and apologize.

As I pushed their doorbell, I saw my hand trembling from nerves. Barry's dad opened the door and motioned us into their living room. Barry and his mom were waiting for us. We all sat opposite each other, and the few seconds of silence that ensued were so awkward it felt like time had stopped. I'd never been in as much trouble, but I knew the truth. I'd never bully anyone intentionally, and I certainly hadn't tried to bully Barry. In that moment, though, it didn't matter. I'd hurt someone else's feelings, which isn't okay, and I knew I had to make the situation right, to rise to the occasion.

I looked down at the ground, then over at my dad, struggling to gain my nerve; and then I took a deep breath, turned to Barry, and said:

"Hey, I'm super sorry. The video wasn't meant to be about you. I didn't mean to make fun of you or make you feel bad in any way."

I stopped and reached out to shake his hand, at which point my dad started to talk to Barry, too.

Back in the truck, my dad wrapped his arm around me the way he did after a football game. "You did the right thing," he said. At school the next day, others, not knowing the backstory, sought me out, wanting to know what happened to the video. "Why'd you delete it?" they asked.

Hindsight is 20/20, and looking back now, I see that I had some growing up to do. Even though I didn't want to at the time, I was forced to learn a lesson, and I'm grateful for that lesson today. Actions have consequences. None of us live in a bubble where our wants and whims are all that matter. Put a check by that box. I didn't leave Barry's house an angel. I was still a kid, a newly minted teenager, and I was still going to mess up . . . a lot.[5]

In the meantime, we kept making videos, some that were funnier, some that were not as funny. But none poked fun at anyone other than me, and believe me, there was, and continues to be, plenty about me to make fun of. Hey, deep down, we're all nerds.

---

5 Wait till you find out the mistake I made in high school that landed me in a place where I knew my future was at stake unless I got my act together.

THE 5 ALL-TIME FUNNIEST ZOOSH VIDEOS

1. "Zoosh Pranks 2"—The traits that define Logan's and my collaborations are on full display in this compilation of antics from a family trip to Florida—physicality and audacious silliness in front of total strangers in public places (e.g., pretending to be stuck in an invisible box at the beach). Serious-minded critics might look at it and go, "Whaaaa?" But hey, look where it got us. ★★★

2. "Zoosh Songs"—Just two guys lip-synching pop songs to each other in a variety of intimate situations. Who knew we could sing so well? But Logan and I may never, ever, ever get back together to do more of these videos. ★★★★

3. "Zoosh Dunks"—This video is of Logan and me dunking on a seven-and-a-half-foot basketball hoop. We edited it with tons of slow-motion action to a score of rap music. It wasn't so much funny as it was cool. It was also pretty funny. ★★★★

4. "Scarred"—This video was our takeoff on the MTV show *Scarred*, a classic that showed skateboarders, daredevil bikers, snowboarders, and dumbass dudes incurring incredible wipeouts from attempted stunts gone wrong. Logan and I survived with only minor bruises. ★★★★

5. "Zoosh Pranks"—I still crack up when I think of myself jumping out from bushes in a crowded shopping area, turning to people

waiting at a crosswalk, and asking, "What year is it?" Or me walking up to someone with a dog and exclaiming, "That's a dog!" Just stupid stuff—but funny. However, in case you want to try this, let me warn you about something: Be prepared to get yelled at, told to go away, or called an idiot, which may or may not be true. Also, you need to be able to run away super fast if necessary—and in more than a few cases, it was. ★★★★

TURN UP THE VOLUME!

ON EVERYTHING.

HITTING THE PAUSE BUTTON

Some perspective is in order. Life wasn't all about making funny videos. Sure it was fun, and they were funny, even hilarious, and we loved making them, but at that time, Zoosh was only a pastime, something my brother and I did to amuse ourselves after we did the stuff that was, in fact, our primary form of fun. For me, that was football. Or FOOTBALL, as I thought of it.

I was super into football. I ate, drank, slept, and woke up thinking about football.

More accurately, I thought about myself starring in an endless loop of ESPN play-of-the-day catches, runs, and end-zone celebrations. That was my fantasy.

My goal was to play in the NFL. By fifth grade, I was doing two hundred push-ups a day, jogging a couple miles, and sprinting up and down the driveway as hard and as fast as possible. I was focused. I got strong. My bedroom walls were decorated with posters of NFL superstars.

When I began playing peewee tackle football in a weekend rec league, I thought it was the start of the rest of my life. My dad and a friend's father coached the team, the 49ers—not to be confused with the actual NFL team—and they instilled a desire to be the best plus a work ethic to match.

My dad was a great coach. For him, the game wasn't all about winning. It was also about building character. At the start of the season, he made every kid look him in the eye, shake his hand, and tell him that he wanted to be part of the team. When you did that, he explained, you were committing to working hard and playing hard.

He had one rule, and I can still hear him say it to the team on the first day of practice: "Don't say the word *can't*. Never say *can't*. Instead, tell me what you *can* do." If a kid didn't shake his hand hard enough, for instance, my dad made him do it again. I pitied the poor kid who said, "I can't shake it any harder, Coach."

"What'd we agree to when you joined the team?" my dad would bark. "We don't say *can't*. We never say *can't*. Give me push-ups."

My dad loved push-ups. He was obsessed with them. He was in the military, and as he explained to Logan and me, "In the army, if you want to get your mail, you have to do push-ups. If you're late, you do push-ups. They motivate. They discipline. They build strength and confidence."

If you wanted to play on his football team, you did push-ups. At the start of every football season, he had the entire team do push-ups at practices. The goal was to do a hundred. Some kids couldn't do ten. But, as he said, they weren't allowed to say *can't*. They had to try.

We did them in increments of fifteen and counted them off as a team. "One, two, three, four . . . fifty-five, fifty-six . . ." As the season went on, everyone on the team, even the kids that had been the weakest at the start, counted them off. Before games, he had us drop and count 'em off. No matter what was going on, everyone—parents, opposing teams, the refs—stopped and watched us. My dad did 'em with us, too. Sometimes we went past a hundred just to show off.

"One hundred eighteen, one hundred nineteen, one hundred twenty . . ."

And no one was louder or prouder than me. I pushed myself on and off the field. I wanted to be the best. I worked myself as hard as I could stand. Then I went home and watched video of myself in games. I'm pretty sure I was the only player who put in that much time and effort. My dad instilled that kind of work ethic; he made it seem normal. The payoff came where it mattered most—on the field.

In junior high, I starred on the seventh-grade team. As much as I loved scoring, the best part was looking at the sideline and seeing my family. My dad had the video camera and Logan cheered me on. It meant a lot to have all of them there, especially my big brother, who was the best athlete in the school. But he had competition coming from his little bro, and he didn't even know it. At the end of the season, I was named a junior all-star.

I spent that summer working alongside my brother, as I had the previous summer, cleaning out old homes for our dad. He supplemented his income as a Realtor by refurbishing fixer-uppers. He'd done this for a few years. During the summers, he put my brother and me to work. The homes were usually in pretty bad shape. Some were disgusting. Our job was to clear out the trash, clean toilets, scrub mold from showers, and sweep spiderwebs and rat droppings from attics and basements. You name it, we did it.

We treated it like a workout. We burned through the demo and clean-up, carrying trash out to a waiting Dumpster as fast as possible. Afterward, we went home and cleaned up, and then Logan and I worked on Zoosh videos. I thought every summer would be like this: helping my dad clean homes, playing sports at the rec center, waiting for football season, and making videos with my brother. I had no reason to suspect anything was going to change, which is generally the way life is when you're a kid—until, you know, things change.

Which was what happened at the end of the summer. As I recall, Logan and I finished working on a house, packed up our tools, and went home for dinner. After cleaning up, my brother dropped the bombshell. He didn't want to make videos anymore. He was going into high school, he explained, and wouldn't have time to work on Zoosh. I was surprised, actually too surprised to debate his decision. We'd never taken Zoosh that seriously; it was something we did for fun, and yet over the past few years we had gained a few thousand followers. Now he was hitting the pause button.

Later that night, he took it even further. We were surfing the Web on our respective computers, as we always did, when he said, "I'm going to delete all the videos." That got my attention. I turned around in my chair and looked at him to see if he was serious. "You want to delete the videos? Our Zoosh videos?"

Logan nodded. He didn't want people in his new high school to see our videos. He wasn't sure they'd think they were cool. My brother had always been the epitome of cool, and he didn't want that to change. So I sort of understood . . . except it was BS. Our videos were popular with thousands of people, and some of those people were in high school. The guys we emulated, like the guys at Smosh, were in high school and college themselves. Those guys were getting famous, and here was Logan getting rid of our videos. I didn't see why he had to take 'em down.

It didn't matter.

Logan was already pressing delete.

I watched without saying a word and then went back to surfing the Web.

In retrospect, I wish I'd protested. Or told him to sleep on it. Or, better still, asked him to wait until school started and see if anyone commented, if anyone thought he wasn't cool. Besides, who cares what people think, anyway? If you like doing something, if you're passionate about it, if it's not hurting people or putting negative energy into the world, I say go for it. Just chase your dreams and don't worry about whether people will think you're cool. If you're doing your thing, you're cool. Period. You don't have to think about it.

I wish I'd said that to my brother.

By the end of the night, he'd deleted 75 percent of the videos on Zoosh. I don't know why he didn't get to 100 percent. I have no idea why he saved some and not others. It was totally random. Of course I'm more upset now about having lost those early videos than I was back then. If I had a time machine, I would go back and tell my brother about the success we were going to have making Zoosh-like videos. All that worrying you do as a kid about little things doesn't seem important when you look back years later. Then again, in reality, Logan and I had other things going on, other things more important than Zoosh.

Like football!

And the season was about to start.

GREG PAUL (MY DAD):
5 THINGS I KNOW ABOUT
JAKE THAT YOU DON'T

1. As a kid, his feet always smelled terribly. They were nasty. If Jake took his shoes off in the car, everyone would want to jump out the window. (I'm happy to report, though, the problem cleared itself up.)
2. He never liked to cut his toenails. Actually, he didn't want to cut them. I'd have to literally hold him down to cut his toenails.
3. Jake was an amazing football player. He had great moves, and most important, he had incredible reflexes. If the ball came close to his hands, he'd do what he needed to do to catch it. I have video of him diving for a pass, doing a twist in the air, and catching the ball one-handed.[6]
4. He always had to be the first one done in class. Whether it was a test or turning in his homework, it didn't matter. He had to

---

6 Hey, it's me, Jake, cutting in on my dad's page. I just want to say I've watched that video at least two hundred times. It is an incredible catch.

be the first one done. He rushed through everything. I'd ask, "What's the hurry? Why don't you use that time to check your work? What are you doing that whole time while everyone else is working?" He'd respond, "I'm sitting there, waiting for class to end."

5. Pass.

ZOOSH-LESS

njuries hampered my eighth-grade football season. I twisted my ankle, then I broke it, and then I broke my finger. The kids were bigger, they hit harder, and I suffered the consequences. I'd go into more detail if there were any worth remembering; it was just a big "forget-it-and-move-on," which I did. Adapt and overcome. Instead of playing basketball, as I had the previous year, I joined the wrestling team. Again, I was following in some pretty large footsteps, in that my dad had wrestled, and my brother wrestled, and both of them wanted me to do the sport hard-core.

So I did.

At 112 pounds, I wasn't the biggest or smallest guy, but I was one of the strongest, and I was possessed by a determination to win. It helped that I'd tagged along to my brother's wrestling tournaments for years and knew some of the moves and the points. Wrestling is based as much on technique as on strength, and it takes time to learn the moves, and then you have to learn how to work them with finesse, while under pressure. Few people are any good when they start, but thanks to all I'd absorbed from watching my brother and the effort I put into practices, I lost only eight matches out of thirty-five my first season, and finished with a third-place trophy.

Unfortunately, I didn't earn any awards in the classroom. My teachers were disappointed in me. On the first day, they expected me to be like my brother, who got straight A's, or A+'s. In the gym *and* the classroom, he went the extra mile. I went that extra mile, sometimes the extra two miles, just not when it came to academics. Despite having the potential to get A+'s, I was a B student—thanks to a C- attention span.

My parents wanted me to live up to my potential. They drove home that message: I had potential, and they didn't want me to waste it. Every time I got a demerit at school, my dad made me do yard work, which wasn't such a bad thing except that he had an enormous yard and I got a lot of demerits; I collected them the way the good students did gold stars. One day I livened up a boring class by doing a funny walk out the door to much laughter. Demerit. Another time I threw a paper ball to a friend two rows away. Demerit. And so on.

Hey, I'm just telling the truth. I was easily bored. I also had a sense of humor and a desire to perform. It was not a good combination over the course of a six-hour school day.[7]

At the midyear point, though, I had to find some self-control or risk missing out on the most-anticipated event of the year: the eighth-grade overnight trip to Washington, D.C. However, you couldn't go on the trip if you had fifteen or more demerits. Fifteen demerits! Most kids went through all of junior high without ever getting one.[8]

I had fourteen.

What can I say?

In my own way, I was an overachiever.

---

7 If any of my teachers read this, I'm sure they'll nod in agreement. I'm sure they'll also be shocked that I've focused long enough to write a book.

8 I'm betting most of you have never got even one.

But I was on my best behavior leading up to the trip. I practiced more self-restraint and relative maturity than at any time in my life. I even impressed myself. Every time I felt the urge to do something funny in class, I asked myself, "WWLD—what would Logan do?" and by the time the trip rolled around, I had managed to stay calm long enough to make it to the capital with my classmates.

Once there, it was a nonstop circus of Zoosh-like behavior, taking place in the shadow of the Washington Monument: I pulled pranks on people, jumped out of bushes, pointed at dogs while screaming, "That's a dog! That's a dog!," pretended to have fallen out of a time machine ("What year is it? Where am I?"), and acted like I was too scared to cross the street.

At night, I was even more animated. We had to be in our rooms by 11 p.m., and the chaperones made sure we were all inside. They taped the outside of the door, and if the tape was broken, they'd know if you snuck out. There was no way to fake it.

To mess with them, the guys in my room and I made a ton of noise. We banged on the walls, on the doors, and yelled for ten to fifteen seconds, long enough so the commotion was heard up and down the floor. Then we stopped. The silence was followed by a knock on the door. We knew who it was without having to look through the peephole. I opened the door, pretending as if I'd just woken up from a deep sleep, and said "Hey, what's up?" to the room attendant. This happened five or six times, always with the same back-and-forth at the door.

"Hey, what's up?"

"There's noise coming from here."

"Only guys snoring," I said.

"No, I heard banging and yelling."

"What? Not from here."

"No, from there," the chaperone said, pointing past me into the dark room.

"Sorry. It's just us sleeping."

"Well, for your own good, sleep a little quieter."

Back home, I hung the better behavior that had gotten me to D.C. in the closet and went back to behaving a little foolishly. One night, while sleeping over at a friend's place with a handful of friends, we snuck out to egg a classmate's house. Sadly, we called this thoughtless behavior fun.[9]

Between the six of us, we had two cartons of eggs and half a plan. As we got close to the house, one guy hurried forward and threw his eggs before the rest of us were ready. The kid's dad heard us and called the cops. One of my friends yelled "Scatter!" and a few people attempted to run, but long story short, we were easily caught and detained while our parents were called, and then my dad, acting as judge and jury, gave me a major grounding.

I wish I could tell you that punishment provided me with an opportunity to search my soul and stop myself from such stupid, impulsive behavior. But I can't lie to you. It didn't. It just felt like a pain-in-the-ass kind of thing, along with extra chores he gave me, since he was super pissed about the incident.

But I was fourteen years old and going to make mistakes. It's part of growing up. You can't learn to walk without falling down. You don't run without tripping once in a while. You don't make prank phone

---

9 I'm sure there are plenty of teens and former teens who already know the way this story goes, because they experienced it themselves.

YOU GOTTA WANT IT

calls without occasionally calling someone who figures out who's on the other end of the line and starts screaming, "Hey, I know who you are and where you live, and I'm going to break that finger you used to dial my number. Do you hear me?" [10]

Bottom line: I missed Zoosh. I had a lot of comedic energy and no place to channel it. And without that outlet, my energy wasn't constructive—it was becoming destructive. I don't deny it: I did a lot of stupid things, and a lot of things I'm not proud of. I was trying to find my path, and without Zoosh, I was a ball of chaos.

So, it's all Logan's fault.

Just kidding.

The truth is, I missed the videos, but at some point toward the end of that eighth-grade year, I experienced something more powerful and consuming than anything else I'd ever experienced in my life. More than wrestling. More than football. More than riding off-road vehicles, which I also loved. No, this thing took over my five senses, all my thoughts, my entire being. It was the distraction of all distractions. It was incredible—and the sudden hold it had over me has never stopped.

I'm sure you can guess what I'm describing here. But you'll have to turn the page to find out for sure.

---

10 Sorry, Dad. I knew you knew it was me.

MY FIRST CRUSH

Though Megan Fox never knew it, I had a relationship with her. It was the summer of 2007, and I went to see the movie *Transformers* with my brother and his friend Anthony at the Crocker Park theaters near our house. I was ten years old, and I thought the movie was the best thing I'd ever seen. I also thought Megan Fox was the hottest girl in this universe. At that age, I knew the word *sexy*, but not its meaning. I can't say that I walked out of the theater thinking Megan was sexy. But I did walk out of the theater thinking *about* Megan, which was something, considering I thought the cars and trucks in that movie were also super hot, and I spent a lot of time thinking about them, too. But for reasons I didn't understand yet, I couldn't get Megan out of my mind. If someone had asked me what I liked about her or why I thought she was hot, I would've said, "She knows how to ride a motorcycle. She's a total badass." She is still a total badass, though our relationship ended. When she was conspicuously missing from the cast of *Transformers 3*, she left me no choice except to move on. But Megan Fox, you'll always be my first love—and we'll both always have *Transformers*.[11]

---

11 Megan, if you read this, DM me.

OWN WHAT YOU DO.
IF YOU DON'T, SOMEONE CAN TAKE IT.

HELLO, LADIES

Girls.

It happened during that eighth-grade year, shortly after returning from the trip to Washington, D.C. I wasn't just noticing girls anymore; I started to like them, too. But that description is not totally accurate. Let me try again. Here's what really happened that year: I started to think about girls nonstop. It was like a light was turned on in the otherwise dark room known as my brain.

No, that's not quite what it was like, either. Instead, picture the Las Vegas strip at night, with all its megawatt neon lights glowing with a blinding brightness in the middle of the otherwise pitch-black desert. No, this is more accurate: It was like God had created the heavens and the earth, and then he got the best idea of all: He created girls. Between that trip and summer, my interest went like this:

girls

Girls

GIRLS

GIRLS!!!

If my life was like this book, everything about girls took over the entire page. Like this:

GIRLS GIRLS GIRLS GIRLS
GIRLS GIRLS GIRLS GIRLS
GIRLS GIRLS GIRLS GIRLS
GIRLS GIRLS GIRLS GIRLS
GIRLS GIRLS GIRLS GIRLS
GIRLS GIRLS GIRLS GIRLS
GIRLS GIRLS GIRLS GIRLS
GIRLS GIRLS GIRLS GIRLS
GIRLS GIRLS GIRLS GIRLS
GIRLS GIRLS GIRLS GIRLS
GIRLS GIRLS GIRLS GIRLS
GIRLS GIRLS GIRLS GIRLS
GIRLS GIRLS GIRLS GIRLS

For some reason, from fifth grade on, girls started to like me. I'd hear gossip that this girl or that girl thought I was cute, which flattered and embarrassed me at the same time. In fifth or sixth grade, it's more awkward than amazing to hear that kind of stuff. What are you supposed to do? Plus, at that age, girls are ahead of boys in that area.

By the summer after eighth grade, though, I caught up. I was like, "Hello, ladies. Where have you been all my life?" It wasn't just awesome to hear that someone thought I was attractive; it was AWESOME. I still didn't know exactly how to react to that type of gossip, and I definitely didn't know what to do if a girl started to flirt with me.

But I was game to find out.

I had a secret weapon to assist me in this new adventure—a cell phone. Though my parents gave it to me in case they needed to get in touch with me or I needed them, in reality, this new cell phone of mine became a digital pipeline to every hot girl I liked. Within the first two days of having it, I was texting ten girls from my school—and they actually texted back!

Make fun of me for what I'm going to say next, but it's the absolute truth: My pants buzzed nonstop, day and night.

At one point, I asked three of them to be my girlfriend. That's not a cool thing to do, I know. Even less cool—I asked all of them in the same week. I made out with two of them in the hallway at different times of day. Then they all found out and were PISSED!

I was both guilty as charged and completely innocent, in terms of intent. I just got caught up in the whole girl scene and went too fast for my own good—or for your own good, as the reader trying to keep track of what my hormones were doing to me. I'll slow down and provide a more detailed picture of what essentially was the onset of puberty.[12]

THE FACTS OF LIFE: At a young age, girls wonder where babies come from. Boys don't. We just accept that there are babies. They come from somewhere. The details are on a need-to-know basis, and we don't need to know. Then, around ages eleven or twelve, girls start wondering not where babies come from, but how they're made. Boys don't get to that stage until a year or two later, as I did, and then we simplify the question to this: What's sex? Sometimes you get a talk from your parents. In my parents' day, it was referred to as "The Talk." From what I understand, it was awkward, it was basic, and then, to the relief of everyone involved, it was over. Done. The Talk was checked off the list and life turned into a ticking time bomb of curiosity and anticipation. For our generation, people like you and me, it's different. We don't get The Talk. Or need it. All we have to do is call up Google on our phone or computer, type in a word or a phrase or a question, and we get the answer. Or we get way more than we bargained for, which was what happened to my friends and me when we got curious. This was all my pubescent pals and I did for a brief moment in our young lives . . . and what an education we got! Through photos and videos, we figured out the basics on our own—and then some—and we were good to go, no Talk necessary. But you don't just walk onto a basketball court and dunk like LeBron James. First, you have to learn to dribble.

---

12 How come *puberty* is acceptable to use in conversation and *pube* isn't?

JENNIFER: One of the popular girls, she was blond and had an athletic body—exactly my type. She was the first girl I ever made out with. We had a crush on each other at a time when both of us were still in that awkward boy-girl stage, and we flirted by text. "You're a loser," she wrote. "You're a loser, too," I wrote back.

At that age, that passed for a deep conversation that translated to: "I like you." "I like you, too." We were in the same classes, and part of a group of friends that hung out together, so there wasn't much to talk about other than who thought who was cute, who liked whom, and other variations on that topic. On weekends, we all gathered at Crocker Park, an outdoor mall with nice stores and restaurants, and public spaces for sitting, talking, texting, and figuring out who liked whom. Every middle schooler went there on Friday and Saturday nights. If you weren't there, you were either sick, out of town, grounded, or being held hostage.

My mom's house was one hundred yards away. I walked there, as did all my friends, including Jennifer.

One night we were at the rec center there. I was playing basketball with friends, and she was hanging out on the sidelines with her posse. We kept looking at each other. Then, during a break in my game, I walked over to her and asked, "Do you have to go to the bathroom? I'm going to the bathroom." She stood up. "Yeah, I have to go to the bathroom, too."

We walked to the bathrooms together, in total silence. There was a men's room, a ladies' room, and a room marked FAMILY. We stood out front for a moment and then, without ever discussing it, we walked together into the shared family bathroom. The door shut, and we stood directly opposite each other. Then we made out.

It was really awkward, in a really wonderful way, and after a few minutes we walked back outside, acting like it had never happened.

Then, a week later, I asked her out—and by out, I mean if she wanted to walk to Crocker Park and hang out with me, the implication being that we could make out again. She said yes.

So did Michele.

Who's Michele?

MICHELE: She was blond and had an athletic body—exactly my type. She just looked sexy. She was the first girl who made me stop everything and go WOW.

So did Julie.

Who's Julie?

JULIE: She was a brunette and had an athletic body—exactly my type. She also had boobs!

This is what happened: I was dating Jennifer, and she changed her status on Facebook to say she was in a relationship, which was the thing to do at the time, but she never told me to do so.[13] I didn't use social media at the time, either. Everyone was on Facebook and Twitter except for me. I was a texter, not a tweeter—and I was texting Michele and Julie, along with Jennifer, though I don't think Michele and Julie knew I was "in a relationship." I don't think I really knew that, either—or if I did, I wasn't sure what that meant in terms of rules and parameters. I do now—don't worry—but then I was naïve and new to this stuff and not thinking rationally.[14]

One day at lunch, Michele sat down next to me and put her hands

---

13 Does that count as an excuse? Let's say it does.

14 I was like a sugar addict in a donut shop.

close to mine. Soon my hand was holding hers, and it stayed that way throughout the entire lunch period. Later, in history class, I texted her about getting together at Crocker Park. When we met up there, I asked, "Do you want to be my girlfriend?"

Charming, right?

And so cool to Jennifer, right?

Michele said yes, and starting that night I had two girlfriends.

This whole time, I was also texting Julie (and her boobs). I was into making out, but I'd heard that others were doing more than kissing, including Julie. I didn't know exactly what she'd done, but thanks to Google, I'd figured out the facts of life, and then some; and so, let's just say my imagination was filled with possibilities: some that seemed potentially realistic and other scenarios that were beyond comprehension.

One Saturday night we were at Crocker Park—me, my friends, and Julie—and we all went back to my mom's house. Julie and I went into my room together and made out.[15] Then, after a while, her hands went places, and so did mine, and suddenly we were past making out, in brand-new territory, at least for me, and I was like, "Oh my God, this is the best moment ever!" The cool thing is, that moment is still pretty great all these years later.

Unfortunately and yet inevitably, the next day, one of my friends told one of Jennifer's and Michele's friends that I'd hooked up with

---

15 One note about this chapter in my life (and book): I realize that I am describing situations that make it seem as if I objectified women. I didn't then, and don't now. These young women were all excellent students, funny, and athletic. Though we might not have discussed world events or literature, we shared insights about the topics that interested us as typical teenagers, like fashion (such as when we walked by the Gap), culinary trends ("Do you think they're handing out free samples at the Wetzel's Pretzels?"), and the latest in digital technology ("Who just texted you?").

Julie. Suddenly the three girls put everything together and I received three separate texts within minutes of each other. All said relatively the same thing: "Wow, you're a player."

Player—that was the word to use when you wanted to call someone a two- or three-timing cheater. But not a dishonest cheater. More of a fun-loving cheater, someone who was unable to resist asking for seconds or thirds. They said, "You're a player." And I was. They were pissed at me, though only for a couple weeks, and then it wasn't like we might never, ever get back together again. They just didn't care anymore. But I did, because suddenly I had a reputation, and it spread across the whole school. From then on, whenever I texted a girl, she replied hesitantly, "People tell me you're a player."

"No," I texted back.

"Well, that's what people say. You're a player."

"Who are you going to believe—them or me?"

"Them."

As I saw it then, I had only one option: to laugh it off and reply honestly:

"I cannot lie. I did have an issue. But I've changed. I've grown up. I'm more mature. And I really like you. So do you want to get together?"

Never mind what the girl responded. I want to ask you, the reader, a question. Does that sound like a player?

GIRLS WHO CAN BE THEMSELVES.
YES! JUST YES!

10 FACTS ABOUT TEENAGE GUYS THAT EVERY TEENAGE GIRL SHOULD KNOW

There are mysteries that really smart people figure out for the rest of us, like cures for diseases, economic forecasts, and ways to battle global warming. Then there are mysteries that beguile all of us, like how does that boat get in the bottle; and then, of course, there's the biggest puzzle of all, the one that begins around the ages of thirteen and fourteen, when people become interested in the opposite sex. That's when the crazy really starts. Anybody who claims to have that figured out is a genius, a poet, or a liar.

I'm none of those, but I am an expert in what it's like to be a teenage guy, so I can speak with tremendous confidence to all of you girls who find boys confusing and distant and even scary, and I can tell you that adolescent guys are none of the above. In fact, they're pretty simple to understand. Picture one of those lightbulbs with three different levels of brightness—dim, bright, and really bright. Guys are like that: They're either sleeping, hungry, or thinking about your . . . Well, here are ten facts about teenage guys that every teenage girl should know:

1. While girls are occupied with their hairstyles, clothes, and shoes, and maybe cool rings and necklaces, most guys in the eighth

grade are thinking about what girls look like after all that's re-moved, and they are in their underwear or bathing suits. They probably don't notice anything more than the color of a girl's hair, if that.

2. By ninth grade, guys are obsessing about what girls look like without their clothes on.

3. Guys at this age may sleep through social studies and look con-fused in math, but they can tell you the name of every girl in junior high who has started to wear a bra.

4. Guys don't have the confidence to pull the first move. So if you like a guy, don't be afraid to be the one to start a conversation and ask for his number.

5. If a guy does like you, play a little hard to get. Kind of tease him. Put him down a little without putting him off. For instance, say, "Those are nice shoes. Did your mom dress you?" Then pause, and add: "Well, even if she did, you still look cute." There was a girl who did that to me and every time she said something like that I'd say to myself, "She's so awesome. She called me a loser. But a cute loser."

6. Make a personal connection. Don't just have conversations over text. Nearly every girl I talked to would text me: "Do you like me?" Or: "Let's hang out." Looking back—and I know this might sound weird coming from a social-media guy like me—I think the most meaningful connections are those made in per-son. Not on your phone, not on Instagram, and not by DMing. It's more satisfying to look into someone's eyes or hear them laugh or see if their hand is inching close to yours, and you can only do that stuff when you are together, in person.

7. Don't worry about rumors. If you like a guy and start talking to him, other people are going to talk amongst themselves, and if

you're in junior high, that talk will very quickly become specu-
lative. People will wonder if you kissed. Someone may even say
they heard you made out. Whatever it is, just brush it off. Ignore
it. Don't let it bother you. Know that people are talking because
they're envious. You're suddenly more interesting than anything
else in their lives, and they'd love to trade places.

8. Ignore cliques and groups. I was in the popular group, and
though it might seem like guys are only interested in girls in their
same group, it's not true. Most guys are interested in anyone
interested in them. Don't be afraid to approach anyone. If a guy
likes you, he likes you, period. Groups and cliques don't matter.

9. Because it was always a thing to hang out in groups, even
through tenth and eleventh grades, I rarely spent any one-on-one
time with girls that I liked. Consequently, I never learned much
about the girl. She'd end up talking with her friends, I'd talk with
my friends, and then the night would be over. So don't be afraid
to break away from the group—you won't miss anything—and
hang out one-on-one.

10. All the things you worry about at that age—your hair, your
clothes, your body—they aren't important. Only one thing matters: YOU. Be yourself. Be authentic. Be honest and honestly
you. And don't worry, that's going to evolve and change as you
discover more about yourself. However, if you are smart, funny,
athletic, like writing code, or are interested in music or food or
something else, be smart, funny, and athletic; create websites; do
whatever it is that makes you uniquely you. Guys will totally like
that. Who you really are is always going to be the most attractive
thing about you.

ADAPT AND OVERCOME

I'm only nineteen years old now—not that old, not that experienced, not that anything, it would seem, to be giving you advice. Yet I'm as knowledgeable as anyone on a topic that everyone goes through: namely, being a teenager. Though I'm not quite finished with these formative years, I can already see the way certain people, events, and even decisions I made have influenced how I got to where I am right now.

Take my dad. If I was a player in high school, he was the original G. I saw the way he was with the ladies, and I was jealous.

Then there was his truck. He drove a Pinzgauer, an enormous, all-terrain military six-wheeler built in the UK. It was manufactured to move troops and supplies in wartime situations. In the suburbs where we lived, it was an attention-getter. When we arrived for football games on Saturdays, everyone in the park knew it. The ground rumbled, heads turned, and kids from every team ran over to get a look, and sometimes a ride. I loved the attention and vowed to have a truck like his when I got older.

He was from a rough area outside of Cleveland, and grew up a tough, wisecracking kid. In high school, he was a jock who got the hottest girl in school, a senior, when he was only a freshman. After graduating, he went into the military, and then got his real-estate license, married, had kids, divorced, and was apparently most comfortable being on his own, though the most important thing in the world to him was being a dad to Logan and me.

As a parent, he emphasized work, focus, and school. He was strict. He always said, "I'm not going to be your friend. I'm going to be your parent, so you better be on top of your sh*t. You can hate me if you want, but one day you're going to thank me."

He was right.

Back in the day, though, I found his rules infuriating, sometimes insufferable. It was his way or the highway. When I was working on one of his homes at 9 p.m., clearing overgrown brush in the dark or cleaning grimy kitchens and wondering when the work would end, while my friends were texting me about hanging out with them at Crocker Park, I hated my dad's hard-ass attitude.

My brother was also a positive influence. He was the person I looked up to and went to for guidance. Logan was always the best at whatever he did. He was an innovator. He was creative and smart. He was funny. Throughout school and in sports, I followed in his footsteps and strove to be as good as him, if not better, which, as I found out, was impossible. Instead, I had to learn to be myself.

That road began the summer before ninth grade, when I stepped onto the field for freshman football practice at Westlake High School. It was hot and the air was thick and heavy. Sweat poured out of me until every inch of my body was drenched. I was covered in dirt and grass, the muck sticking to me. Guys around me complained and groaned. Some puked.

I'm not painting a pleasant picture, but then, it wasn't supposed to be. It was, by design, miserable. Everything hurt and everything sucked, which is what two-a-day workouts during summer football feel like. Guys quit by the handful every day. We began with sixty players, and after two months, less than half were still on the field and I was one that stayed. Every day I dug in harder. My brother was already a star on the varsity; I was out to prove myself.

I'd never done anything as rigorous. In practices, the coach pushed us harder and longer than the varsity. He wanted us to be the best. He drilled it into us that we were not playing just for him but to inspire future generations of players. If we won, they'd work to maintain the school's reputation as winners. In some ways, he reminded me of the way my dad had coached us.

Two months into the season, the coach said something that turned into one of the most valuable lessons I ever learned. It was after school, during a practice, and he was putting the offensive linemen through drills. He gave one of the guys a specific instruction, which didn't work out. Either the player didn't execute properly, or his defensive counterpart blocked his move. The coach blew the whistle, and said, "You screwed up! What happened?"

"You told me to go to my right, but then he went the other way and—"

The coach cut him off.

"Okay, I understand. It didn't work out. So adapt and overcome."

The player nodded. Understood.

But was it? The coach wanted to make sure. He faced the entire team and waited a moment, allowing everyone to settle and focus.

"Did you all see what happened? Did you follow? Let me explain in case you weren't paying attention. We had a play. It didn't work out. Why didn't it work out? Because someone on the other side did something unexpected. Gentlemen, that happens all the time. That is what we call life. Not just football but life. The unexpected happens all the time. What are you supposed to do? You are supposed to think. You are supposed to adapt. You are supposed to overcome. Adapt and overcome. If you learn anything this season, learn that—adapt and overcome. There's no set way to do something in life—ever. So what do you do? You adapt and overcome. Adapt and overcome . . ."

I applied that lesson throughout high school. Midway through the season, my ankle gave out and sidelined me for the remainder of the games. I was miserable, but gradually the time out proved an eye-opener. I recognized that my goal of playing in the NFL wasn't realistic. I wasn't big enough; I didn't go to a school with an athletic program that fed into Division 1 colleges; and I wasn't enjoying the game as much as I had before, when the biggest objective was to have fun.

Though I stayed on the team, I branched out—my way of adapting and overcoming—by exploring other interests. I talked to everyone in school, from the musicians in the marching band to the kid who ate lunch by himself, buried in a book. I was like Curious George—always sticking my nose into something, always asking questions. I asked teachers how they picked test questions. I asked seniors what college they were going to and how they did on their SATs. I wanted to know how the band director decided who marched where. How was that order determined?

Outside of school, I was obsessed with *Rob Dyrdek's Fantasy Factory*. It was the only TV show I watched regularly (and six years later I went to the factory, which was sick; and I have pictures!). *Fantasy Factory* was partly about his business, partly about skateboarding and having fun, and partly about Rob hanging out with celebrities—it truly was the fantasy life for so many kids like me. And like me, he was from Ohio. He was focused on success, and living his ultimate dream, and the show let us see him in action. I was the kid watching at home who thought, *He's just like me. He's even from my home state. How can I do what he's doing?*

So there I was in ninth grade, starting to figure out who I was and who I wanted to be, with the help of awesome influences:

1. My dad
2. My mom
3. Logan
4. My football coach
5. Rob Dyrdek
6. Josh Pappas

Who's Josh Pappas? Josh was my practice partner all through the eighth-grade wrestling season. He was also the best junior high wrestler anyone had seen in years. In Ohio, amateur wrestling occupies a status on a par with most pro sports, and Josh was a superstar. Since I was just starting out in the sport, I wanted to be as good as him, if not better. In practices, I made sure to work harder than him. I sprinted faster. I tried to lift more weight than him. Whatever it was, he set the bar high and I tried to go even higher. By the end of the year, I was voted hardest worker and most improved. And Josh? He did the unheard-of—he went undefeated.

Then in ninth grade the two of us went out for wrestling and were the only freshmen that made the team. The roster was composed of fourteen kids, including my brother. Logan's picture was constantly in the local newspaper, the *Morning Journal*, as the team's star. It was the first time we had been on a team together, and I was psyched. I'd never gotten to see him work in practice. I'd always been one of the hardest workers on my team, but now my brother and the others were busting ass at a whole different level, and I had to strain to keep up with them.

I went into the opening match of the season feeling confident— maybe too confident, even slightly cocky. It was my second season wrestling, and I'd been working hard. As I stepped onto the mat, I told myself, "You got this. It's going to be easy work. Quick work."

But it wasn't easy—at least for me. Within minutes, my opponent pinned me and the match was over. BAM. Just like that. He totally destroyed me. I'd never lost that badly in anything. Here's the thing about it: Just as certain people influence our lives, there are also moments that define who we are and determine who we will become in the future, and for me, this loss was one of those moments.

In fact, as I think about it now, I'd say it was *the* moment.

I knew what it was like to lose. I'd lost in football, but that was a team sport. I'd lost wrestling matches, too. Only a handful of them. But that was back in eighth grade, my first year of competition, and I didn't expect much of myself. I'd also gotten my ass kicked a few times the previous summer when I took up boxing and MMA. But again, I was a novice, with no experience and fewer expectations.

This first match of the season was different. I wanted to win. I thought I was going to win handily. I'd worked hard in the gym, felt strong and smart, and put a lot of pressure on myself to walk away with a victory. Instead, I got my ass kicked. I lost—badly.

In one way or another, every teen has moments like this one, whether it's a bad grade, getting teased, waking up with zits, feeling like you aren't cool, hearing some lame excuse after asking a girl out on a date, not getting asked to a dance, or getting trounced in a wrestling match you expected to win. The list is a long one, but it all feels the same—like the floor has caved in, like life is one giant sinkhole.

I got up off the mat, shook my head till I was clear-eyed, and then sat back on the bench, burying my head in a towel. My teammates offered words of encouragement.

"Next time, man."

"Good try. You'll get your turn again."

"Forget about it."

"Brush it off. Look to the next one."

I heard their words but still disappeared inside myself searching for my own inner voice, the one that would enable me to lift my head out of my towel and begin to feel better. At first, like everyone, I only heard the negative stuff. I was hurting. But then the real me started to come through, and I heard my inner voice speak. The words were loud and clear.

Adapt and overcome.

I said those words to myself and have said them many times since. Not every video gets a million views. Not every project works out. Not everyone wants to Like or Friend me. Life is full of challenges, mistakes, rejections, and defeats, and those are the times when we learn the most, not just how to correct our mistakes or leap over obstacles. We also learn about ourselves, what we're made of. I know I did—and have continued to learn. I listen for that inner voice that tells me to get up, to brush off the pain, and to adapt and overcome.

At the next practice, my partner, Andrew, the team captain, beat my ass as he did in every practice. He was lighter than me, but super strong, and he had near-perfect technique. He wasn't team captain for nothing. Losing like that, time after time, was a lot for me to handle. However, it made me tougher. It made me work harder, to the point where I might not have beaten him, but I competed with him at a higher level than before. I got better.

As the season went on, I still lost a bunch of times, but I also won my share of matches. I found my way. We competed from November to March. When the season wrapped, Josh and I were the only freshmen to get varsity letters. It was pretty cool. Even better was the sense that I had grown, that I'd met challenges head-on and gotten past them. I realized that for me, there was something even more important than winning. It was the satisfaction I got from learning new things, from testing and pushing myself, from turning the possibility of failure into . . . well, an opportunity to see what happens if I try.

And that's still the way it is.

THE *YOU GOTTA WANT IT* PLAYLIST—TOP 5

’m in the gym. Or I'm on my hoverboard, getting around Hollywood. Or I'm in my truck, heading to the set. Or I'm getting ready
to meet up with friends. I want to feel psyched, feel motivated, feel
that surge of energy and power I get when I'm lifting and pushing
myself to do more than before. For me, music is a key ingredient in
summoning that kind of inner strength and focus. Here are the songs
on my playlist that get me to that place:

1. "Started from the Bottom," by Drake
2. "Ima Boss," by Meek Mill, featuring Rick Ross
3. "Forever," by Drake, featuring Lil Wayne, Eminem, Kanye West
4. "Put On," by Young Jeezy, featuring Kanye West
5. "MegaMan," by Lil Wayne

GRIIIIIIIND!

THERE'S NO OTHER WAY.

REALLY, TRULY STUPID BEHAVIOR

Raise your hand if you've done something stupid—I'm talking really, truly stupid. I'm going to stop typing for a second in order to raise both of my hands. Hang on . . .

Okay, I'm back—and here's a list of some of the things that caused me to raise my hands:

- During recess in sixth grade, I was playing football with my best friend. He was on the other team. We got into an argument and he attacked me and I fought back. It wasn't a serious fight, but the teacher supervising the yard thought it was and both of us got suspended for a day. It was the first time I got in trouble. I felt like an idiot.
- One day in seventh grade, I fell asleep in geography class. The teacher had one of those strict, direct, and sarcastic personalities that made him both famous and feared by all students, even those who weren't yet in junior high. You either loved him or hated him. As for me, let's just say neither of us would've joined an admiration society for the other. The day I fell asleep, he snuck up behind me and smacked a long wooden pointer on my desk. I sprang up, startled by what sounded like a gunshot, and we had an exchange along these lines:

  "Good morning, Mr. Paul. Rough night?"

"Yeah, I'm not feeling well."

"You're not feeling well and took time to fall asleep in my class? How special. Michael Jordan played in the NBA championships with a 102-degree fever. He was sick, and he won the championship."

"But he was paid $30 million. I'm not getting anything here."

He shook his head, suddenly silenced, though I never knew if it was because I got the best of him or he thought the worst of me.

- In eighth grade, I helped some friends egg a house. This was before the time the cops caught and detained us, and I'm purposely not going to say anything more about it because I don't know the statute of limitations on acting like a jerk.

- That same year, I also helped some friends T.P. a house (address purposely withheld, because again, I don't know the statute of limitations on being a jerk).

Once, when I was on a tour, several fans asked me to describe my worst day of high school, and I flippantly said, "Every day was the worst," which played well to that crowd. But it was an exaggeration. Every day wasn't the worst. Some days were definitely worse than others. It depended on the class, the situation, and the grade.

My freshman year was boring, and my junior year was dreary, and my grades reflected a lack of interest. I got B's and B+'s. I could've gotten A's, but I applied myself just enough to keep my parents satisfied that my life wasn't headed toward the gutter.

It's torture to sit in a classroom without any interest in the subject—and that's exactly what it was like for me in French class. Every time, on my way to class, I had the same experience: I would be hurrying to the room, trying not to be too late, and suddenly I would stop and say to myself, "Oh crap, I forgot to do my French homework!" The teacher was a stickler. She began every class by asking to see our homework. Literally, she had us hold it up in the air while she walked around the room, eyeballing the papers from afar.

Could she actually see what was on the paper?

A short ways into the term, I began playing the odds. Instead of worrying about doing my homework, I wrote a bunch of random words on a piece of paper—*elephant, taco, Megan Fox, I hate French*— and kept it in my backpack. When the teacher called for homework, I got out the paper and raised it along with everyone else's, only I held mine like the flag of a triumphant hero. Then one day, she collected the papers.

"Oh crap," I said under my breath.

She heard me—sort of.

"En français, s'il vous plaît, Monsieur Paul," she said.

I shrugged.

"Oh *crapez* . . ."

I got a laugh, but that was about all.

My poor attitude grew out of boredom. I just didn't connect with school at that time, and when you are like that, you float around until you find something or someone that you do connect with—like when I became friends with a couple guys who, like me, were out of sync with the mainstream.

Eddie and Phil were in my grade, and they were clever, funny, and high-energy guys, and always scheming about something, which made them exciting to hang out with.

Unfortunately, their schemes tended to take advantage of people. They made fun of kids and played pranks, which made them feel like big shots, and for some stupid reason I got caught up in their shenanigans.

Especially this one time that resulted in really, truly stupid behavior—the worst thing I've ever done. I don't want to tell this story. It's total cringe material. I wish I could expunge it from my memory. The only reason I'm sharing this particular incident is the hope that it can serve as a cautionary tale to those out there who, like me at that age, have an inner jerk that needs a good slap-down. Or maybe do what I failed to do: Listen to your inner voice when it tells you that you're being driven down the wrong road.

Anyway, here's what happened: I was at school one day and closing my locker when Eddie and Phil came up and told me to follow them around the corner. There, Eddie pulled out an iPhone and Phil bragged that they had just taken it from a kid.

"It's worth like four hundred dollars," he said.

"More," Phil added.

I should have told them that was wrong, walked away, and reported them for stealing. I didn't. I stood there, staring expressionlessly at the phone, and then at them, as if to say, "So what?" I balanced my books and notebook under my arm and then took a step toward my next class, down the hall.

"We're going to steal another one," Eddie said.

I shrugged off that statement and kept walking. The next day, they showed me another phone, explaining they'd taken it from a kid in a crowded hallway as people were hurrying between classes. They high-fived each other and laughed at their victim for not even realizing what they'd done. Then they turned serious.

They told me about the money they expected to make selling these stolen iPhones to a guy they knew who resold them for double to someone with an electronics store in a nearby suburb, and they said if I wanted in on the money, I had to help them. I wasn't about to steal anything, but under pressure of being kicked out of their crew, as they phrased it, I met up with them a couple days later and helped distract a younger student while they took his phone. We met up afterward.

"That was so easy," Phil said, laughing and looking at me as if expecting a similar reaction.

I said nothing. I felt awful. I wanted to get away from these guys.

Two days later, Eddie and Phil stole another kid's iPhone, and Phil forgot to turn it off. The phone was traced, and the cops were called. They showed up at Phil's house ready to arrest him. Apparently they had already connected him to the other iPhones that had been reported stolen from the school, and from what I heard later on, Phil confessed to everything immediately. He told them Eddie was his partner in crime, and he identified me as an accomplice.

During school the next day, I was summoned to the principal's office. I was not a total stranger to the chair opposite the principal's desk, but never for anything more serious than cracking a joke or having my cell phone on and texting in class—basically my most serious offenses at school stemmed from being bored, immature, and disruptive, not anything close to being criminal.

This time, however, I walked into the principal's office and found not one but three men waiting for me: the principal, the assistant principal, and a uniformed police officer. I froze before even letting go of the door handle, trying to figure out what was going on. The office was still and quiet and filled with a sense of gravity. As the door closed behind me with a heavy thud, I knew something bad was about to happen, and though I went into a kind of shock, I think things unfolded pretty much like this:

The principal motioned for me to sit, which I did.

"Do you know why you've been called here?" he asked.

"No," I said, though as soon as I said it, I put everything together, and saw myself back in the hall, distracting that kid while Eddie and

Phil took his phone. I felt sick and scared and wanted to disappear. The cop stepped forward and explained that my friend Phil had told him that I was involved in stealing iPhones.

I wanted to correct him and explain I had only distracted one kid, in a single incident, and I felt terrible about it, but there was no need for me to say anything, as the assistant principal then recounted the entire incident involving me and "the student victim," as he called him.

The principal spoke next, and with tremendous disappointment in his voice, as opposed to the sternness of the others, he merely said, "Jake?"

"I did it," I said.

For the next half hour, I answered questions and confirmed every detail of the iPhone thefts. Those thirty minutes seemed to last longer than my entire life. They felt, in fact, like the end of my life, especially when both the principal and assistant principal mentioned the possibility of expulsion. In retrospect, I know they wanted to teach me a lesson, and knew my heart was pounding so hard I could feel it against my chest. I was only a freshman, and they wanted to make sure I didn't go any further down the wrong path, and, in fact, turned around and started back on the right path.

They called my mom, who freaked out when they explained the reason I was sitting in the principal's office with a policeman. "He's not allowed to get in trouble," she said loud enough for me to hear through the receiver. She wanted to kill me. She didn't have to, because my dad was more than happy to carry out the execution once they called him.

"Jake, is this true?" he asked me later that afternoon.

"Yes, sir," I said.

He just stared at me. It was the first time in my life that I felt the full impact of silence—that silence equals death.

There was a lot of discussion between my parents and the principal, and ultimately I avoided expulsion—but not punishment, which included a ten-day suspension from school, a court session in front of a judge, and forty hours of community service. But there was more. At home, my dad gave me the most serious, straightforward lecture of my life, which went like this: "Jake, you have every opportunity to succeed in life. You're a good kid. But you're doing stupid sh*t. That's your choice, and if you want to go down that path, I have to let you know what it's going to be like. I want you to experience life doing hard labor."

My dad, being the no-nonsense way he is, let me experience hard labor. Every year at this time, he split the equivalent of two cords of firewood by hand and gave it to neighbors for Thanksgiving. Two cords of firewood is a lot—enough for a neighborhood. My dad said I was to spend the weekend carrying it from the backyard to the front, a distance of about two football fields, and on Saturday morning, when I started, it was pouring rain, and cold. I didn't stop until it was dark, and then I continued on Sunday, from morning till dark again. By the time I deposited the last few logs in front, my entire body ached more than after any football game or wrestling match I could ever remember. I was spent.

That was my dad's point.

He wanted me to feel the pain—and I did.

I had a hard time going back to school following my suspension. Everybody knew what had happened, and many people now regarded me as a bully. I'd relished a reputation as a star athlete, a class clown, and even a player with the ladies. I didn't want to be known as a bully. That wasn't me. I was a good guy. I remember going into court and saying as much to the judge who'd assigned me community service. I was full of remorse, and it was obvious that I meant it.

"If you stay out of trouble for the next six months, I'll take this off your record," he said. "But you should really thank your dad. Most kids like you from the suburbs call a lawyer, they pay a fine, and they walk out without ever having a second thought about what they did. But I saw the pictures your dad took of you moving firewood. I know because of what he had you do you're going to think long and hard about ever making another mistake. So get out of here—and be good."

I didn't need to hear that twice. From then on, I stayed on the straight and narrow and did whatever I could to reverse people's impression of me. It took a long time for me to come to terms with this event. I'd think about it and ask myself, "What the hell were you thinking?"

Obviously, I wasn't thinking. But I did afterward. I dropped Phil and Eddie as friends and learned the lessons I needed to learn. Every kid is going to do something stupid. You're going to get in trouble. It's the way we learn to stay on the road; you hit the wall, you nick the car next to you, and then you figure out how to stay in your lane or parallel park without banging into your neighbor's car. It's part of growing up.

Listen, here's my final point: It's not okay to do bad things to other people. But it is okay to make mistakes, and you will make them as you grow up. Don't beat yourself up when that happens. Instead, wake up, take stock of whatever happened, and then take the steps to not make the same mistakes, to learn from them. For me, that meant not ever again giving in to, or even worrying about, peer pressure. From then on, the only pressure I dealt with was the pressure I put on myself to be the best at those things that were important to me—and I'm still doing that.

In fact, I'm still doing really, truly stupid things now, but they're really funny, and I'm really good at 'em—and I record them! Instead of hurting other people, my antics make them laugh.

Be a good person, and good things will happen.

5 THINGS I WISH I'D KNOWN AT 15

1. Though it may not seem like it, life gets better if you want it to—and work at it.
2. Homework, acne, thinking you don't have the right shoes, why doesn't he/she call, all the things that get you down as a teenager, they don't really matter—you just don't know it yet.
3. Girls are great, and they get even better as they grow up.
4. School may suck, but that doesn't mean there aren't classes and instruction out there that will inspire you in ways your teachers don't. I wish I'd known about online courses in business, accounting, marketing, comedy, acting—things that got me excited later on when I found out they existed.
5. Math is more important than I thought.
6. When you're a teenager, the world is basically school and your bedroom. In reality, it's a lot bigger than that. Not only in the physical sense but in terms of possibilities. The only limitation is your imagination. You can live anywhere. You can do and be anything.
7. You gotta want it.[16]

---

16 I know, this is No. 7 on a Top 5 list. I *told* you math is important.

ZOOSH 2.0

When scholars write the history of funny videos on social media, as they no doubt will, and wonder what was going on in the lives of the Paul brothers when they decided to bring back Zoosh, they're going to be surprised to discover that nothing was going on, absolutely nothing.

This was key. If you're fifteen or sixteen years old and fully booked with extracurricular activities, lessons, and volunteer work—all the stuff that fills out a college application to go along with a 3.95 GPA—you're never going to have the free time needed to sit on the couch, where you can come up with the idea to go to the grocery store, jump into a stranger's cart, and yell, "For Narnia!"

I must point out that period of inspired nothing-going-on-ness was preceded by months of industry and effort. The summer between ninth and tenth grades, I worked alongside Logan in a landscaping business that he started. I can still picture myself at the end of hot, sticky afternoons, gulping gallons of water as I stood by his car, exhausted, shirtless, sweaty, and covered with mulch that burned and itched my skin. Flies swarmed around me, as if I were an all-you-can-eat buffet.

Mulching was the worst, and everyone wanted us to do it. But the worst job brought out the best in us. We dove in and worked hard, knowing there was a reward at the end of the day—money! Credit goes to my dad for pushing us to be self-starters and reliant in our own business, rather than getting a minimum-wage job like all of our friends. He said we would learn real-life skills.

"You'll have to communicate with adults," he explained. "You'll negotiate prices. You'll budget your time and keep to a schedule. You'll learn to be responsible for the quality of your work and the way your reputation depends on it. You can charge as much as the market will bear. And you'll have cash at the end of the day."

We were sold. Logan made flyers, wrote a brief description of our services—mow lawns, blow leaves, rake, cut hedges, edge, mulch, everything needed to make your yard look good—and our price ($10/hr. per person). He passed them out and posted them on bulletin boards at local stores. My mom and dad both gave them out at their offices, too. Within days, people called and we were in business.

From the start, it was clear we were different. We didn't just work hard, we sprinted as we worked, going as fast as we could, treating the different tasks like a workout. It's funny to think back on the way some of our clients came outside to inspect the work, scratching their heads as they said, "You're already done? So fast?" Other clients—moms and their older daughters—came outside just to inspect us. Tanned and cut, we worked with our shirts off, in shorts, with sweat pouring off our bodies.

Once school started, wrestling took over both our lives—especially mine. Logan was already a star. Since he was a senior, he wanted to crush the entire season, and he did. He didn't lose until his twentieth match. I got a lot better, too. I lifted weights and worked out every day after school and worked harder than ever during practices, where my teammate Josh also pushed me. Strong and confident and more experienced, I started the season losing only one of my first six matches. Better than winning was the realization that I was improv-

ing, that all the work was being rewarded. As the season wore on, Josh
and I had the same record, 15-4, and I ended up qualifying for the
districts—one of only four guys on the entire team to go that far!

"Dude, we're both going!" my brother exclaimed in the gym after I
clinched my spot with a victory.

"It's insane!" I replied, with a towel draped around my shoulders,
huffing and puffing, physically spent in a way that made me feel on
top of the world.

Districts were double elimination. I won my first match but lost
my second one. Two of the other kids on our team lost right away.
That left Logan and me carrying the rest of the team, which was cool.
Then I won another match, improving my record to 2-1. Unbeliev-
ably, I won the next one, too. Four wins got you to state. I was going
crazy with excitement, jumping up and down, trying to stay focused.
In Ohio, if you tell someone you went to state in wrestling, they're
like, "Oh sh*t!"

Which was what I was saying to myself and anyone else nearby on
the sideline. Logan got his fourth win just before I walked onto the
mat for my final match. I was super proud of him and thinking magic
was about to happen to me, that I had a shot at something completely
surreal, and that both my brother and I might go to state—that is,
until I found out my opponent was the previous year's state champion. With a couple of slick moves, he brought me back to reality, and
I lost. I was out. But my brother went on to state, where he took fifth
place!

Away from the gym, Logan's amazing senior year continued. He
blitzed the SAT and ACT tests, and got accepted by all five colleges he
applied to. In the end, he got a full-ride academic scholarship to Ohio
University. My parents celebrated even more than when he'd done so
well at state. By spring, he was biding his time till graduation, done

with sports, and thinking only about his future at OU. He was talking about which courses he wanted to take and which subjects interested him as possible majors. Nothing else was going on—and looking back, I think he was simply bored the night he approached me with the suggestion that changed both of our lives.

"Dude, what're you doing?" he asked.

I looked up from the TV. At that moment, I was playing Call of Duty, as I did most nights. My routine was school, lifting, watching YouTube videos, and playing Call of Duty.

"I'm playing Call of Duty."

"But what are you doing?"

"Nothing. Why?"

"Let's start making some videos again," Logan said.

"All right. That sounds fun. I'm down. Let's do it."

Logan offered a fist. I pounded it.

"We're getting a better camera first," he said.

"Definitely."

The next day we drove to Best Buy and found the coolest guy in the camera department. We were honest with him.

"We need a lens that zooms in really far so we can prank people," I said.

He smiled. "We're going to hook you up."

After a couple hours of discussion, questions, joking around, and imagining a variety of situations, we left with a Canon DSLR camera, a powerful lens, and a wireless mic. Logan and I split the cost. The money came from our landscaping earnings. Once home, we began thinking of ideas. They came fast and furious, just like before. We laughed and checked out favorite videos from other people on You-Tube. It was exciting to feel the charge of our creative energy again.

For our first video with the new camera, we re-created "Zoosh

Songs," our lip-synching masterpiece. It was among the ones Logan had deleted three years earlier, and also one of the funniest. It was fitting that we did it again first for Zoosh 2.0. We planned out the songs and shot it throughout my mom's house, starting in the basement, moving upstairs to her room, and finishing with my brother jumping out of a second-story window.[17]

Actually, we added another thirty seconds after he landed on the front walk. We had too many songs we wanted to do, and we kept adding ideas that made us laugh. By the next day, we had posted it on YouTube and got to three thousand views pretty quickly. Even though Zoosh had been dormant for three years, we still had about four thousand subscribers, and many of them, it seemed, clicked on the new video. This type of welcome back would've been enough for most people. Logan and I didn't know what "enough" meant. We were natural athletes and competitors, and our inclination in whatever we did was to always push for more and better. Three thousand views were great, but we wanted more.

"I have an idea," Logan said. "Let's upload it to iFunny."

iFunny was an app for funny videos. They featured new videos a few times a day. We checked out videos there all the time, exploring the depth and breadth of the content people posted as well as those in the featured slots. Those in the featured slots had the most views. As far as we were concerned, though, they weren't always the funniest.

"It probably won't get featured," Logan continued.

"But maybe it will," I said.

---

17 Me researching this part of the book: "Mom, how could you let him jump out the window?"
My mom: "He was very athletic. I knew he could do it."
Me: "You're a little crazy."
My mom: "Where do you think you get it from?"

My brother posted our video, and we watched and waited to see if it would get featured. It didn't. Later that day, he caught up with me after school.

"Yo, what if we posted it a bunch of times?" he wondered.

Good question. Logan immediately posted and reposted the video until he received a message saying he'd reached the maximum number of posts allowed that day under his account. I then opened an account of my own and posted it as many times as allowed. Both of us did the same thing the next day, posting like ten or fifteen times. Following a short wait period, we noticed the views went up significantly, to between a thousand and three thousand views. They kept going up, too. The next day we made two additional accounts. Between all our accounts, we posted that video thirty or forty times. Each time, the views rose. It was great, like pumping water into the ground and seeing oil come shooting back up.

The next week, literally the week after we got the camera, we went on vacation to Siesta Key, Florida. My mom wanted to celebrate Logan getting into college, along with his academic scholarship. I was into that; why not spend some of the money being saved on tuition sending me to the beach? Logan and I brought the camera, intending to film some pranks. By the time we arrived at the hotel, we were loaded with ideas. We made the entire week about pranks, reprising some of our old work—for instance, me jumping out of bushes into a crowd at the crosswalk, seemingly lost and confused as I yelled, "It's worked! What year is it?" I also shot Logan from afar at the beach, as he jumped over unsuspecting sunbathers. Once, as he jumped over four girls lined up on their towels, he clipped the last girl.

"Not funny!" she yelled.

Others offered variations on the same theme.

"Really?"

"Douchebags."

"You guys are dumb."

"Don't film me!"

"You know what? You're an ass."

"F— off!"

As every prankster knows, it got even funnier when one of those people who didn't think we were funny confronted us—well, it was usually me they confronted, because Logan was across the way with the camera.

"Why are you being such an ass?"

"What do you mean?" I said.

"You know what I mean?"

"I can't understand. I don't speak English."

"You and that guy there—your brother—I see you."

"No you don't. We're invisible."

"You have a camera."

"No we don't."

"Both of you. You and you."

"That's not even us."

As we went back to the hotel, we couldn't stop laughing. Then we laughed even harder watching the video. Once back home, we edited the footage and posted it on iFunny multiple times, via our various accounts. The video went viral in our school. Everyone watched it and thought it was the funniest thing they'd seen. Kids I didn't even know came up to me in the hallway and said, "Yo, that was so funny. You guys are insane." Even the teachers watched it. Several admitted to Logan and me that they thought it was laugh-out-loud funny. One teacher even said, "It was LOL"—which made me LOL.

"Have you ever heard anyone say 'LOL' before?" I asked my brother, still howling at the total awkwardness of this teacher trying to sound in the know. But hey, it was great that so many people were laughing.

The reaction and the attention motivated us to keep making videos. We made one every week or two, when the idea was right and we had the time. We weren't obsessed yet. Though the volume of content on Zoosh grew steadily, our followers stayed about the same, increasing by maybe five or ten a day but nothing too radical. That wasn't the point. We were still more into amusing ourselves than entertaining anyone else, which is the way you should be when starting out on something like this. You have to be passionate about whatever it is you're doing. It can't seem like work, and it has to come from a pure place. And it did with us.

But then something happened that changed the game.

I DON'T MIND A CHALLENGE.

SERIOUSLY. BRING IT.

6 SECONDS

It was a new video app. It was easy to download, easy to use, and the videos it let you make lasted only six seconds. It was called Vine, and I thought it was about the coolest thing I'd ever seen. Figuring out how to create and cram a joke into just six seconds was super fun. Unfortunately, no one else was on it, and only a few outside obsessives and geeky early adapters and guys like me had even heard of it. So for a budding attention-seeking jokester, it was a quick nonstarter.

Hello, Vine.

Goodbye, Vine.

It sat on my phone like someone you go out with a couple times and with whom, despite the two of you having a good time and a lot in common, nothing happens—at least until you see one of your friends going out with them.

And so it was with Vine and me. Until . . .

A few months later, everyone was talking about Vine. It was one of those things where seemingly overnight, everyone was downloading Vine and talking about it. I recognized an opportunity. Vine was perfect for my sense of humor, and the landscape was wide open. I made a sh*t-ton of Vines and watched eagerly as my "likes" grew. It was a thrill to get more than ten; starting with the eleventh like, they changed from names to numbers, indicating that, more than friends, you had a following.

Within days, I had fifty followers. Most were from school, but friends told other people, and then they shared, and soon I had what I'd long desired: an audience. It was addictive. I wanted to keep growing that number. At the same time, I felt a responsibility to entertain everyone with good videos. Anyone could make a Vine, but it took thought, planning, and work to create and execute a video that was actually funny.

And Vine was all about one take in six seconds. There was no editing. If I wanted to do something to music, I had to play it and time everything perfectly. The same was true with sound effects. Every video required numerous takes to get those six seconds exactly the way I wanted.

I remember my mom watching me obsess over a video and wishing I put as much effort into my schoolwork. What can I say, other than I liked making videos more than doing homework, and also playing to an audience. I loved the way it felt when someone complimented my Vines or said they were funny. My teachers might've said that about some of my test scores (ha-ha),[18] but if people had been able to follow me in history or click "Like" on my tests, I might've tried harder.

I told Logan about Vine and showed him some of my Vines. He started making them, too, but not as seriously or as frequently as me. He was a scholarship collegian while I was a class clown; guess which one of us took to Vine instantly? Then, one day, Logan and his girlfriend watched me shooting a Vine. A friend of mine was there, too. After I did several takes, my brother suggested trying it another way.

"It'll be funnier," he said.

I disagreed, and we got into an animated debate about whose idea

18 Admittedly, some of my test scores were pretty funny.

was funnier, what made something funny, and which one of us was funnier. It was typical brother-collaborator stuff, done in front of our friends, with both of us citing favorite YouTube videos as evidence of what was truly funny, until finally I said, "Yo, I know what I'm talking about. I have more followers than you."

That stopped him. It was hard to argue against the data.

His expression changed. I knew exactly what he was thinking. Suddenly, it was game on.

Starting the next day, he began studying Vine. He learned everything about how to make Vines, how to post them, and how to get people to like them—or, as he said, "How do I get more followers than Jake?"

For a smart, social-media-savvy, and funny guy like my brother, it was easy. Within three days, he had more followers than me. We're talking fifty people at this point, but still. I said, "Whoa, I can't let this happen."

Both of us put a lot of effort into making our Vines the funniest. It was no different than when we played one-on-one basketball. We were the friendliest of adversaries, like competitive collaborators, sharing ideas and helping out with effects, but each of us wanted to win.

Two weeks later, we shot a Vine that became our first mega-hit. At the time, you had to press the screen nonstop to record a Vine. It wasn't possible to set up your phone anywhere, stop and start, upload clips, or anything else. You simply shot for six seconds and then sent out the Vine in search of followers. But on this particular day, Logan was at my mom's house, trying to make a Vine. My cousins Alli and Matt were there, too. Logan wanted me to drop the phone down the stairs and then he'd catch it at the bottom, capturing the stunt from the phone's point of view.

After several unsuccessful attempts (I can still hear his frustrated

cursing—"Dammit, I can't do it because I can't let go of the button"),
Alli suggested using the iPhone's assistive touch feature, a setting that
mimics a finger touch when you have a broken screen.

"It'll be like hacking Vine," she said.

It was exactly like that—and it worked. Brilliantly. On the video,
I dropped the phone, the phone fell, and Logan caught it at the bottom. Nothing like that had ever been done before on Vine. Very soon
after the video was posted, within hours, it went viral. For two days,
it was No. 1 on Vine's most popular/viewed list. It had something like
four million views and fifty thousand likes. Those numbers were insane. Before then, our videos got in the neighborhood of eleven likes
and maybe seventy-five views. This wasn't just a new neighborhood; it
was a new universe.

Logan got five thousand followers from posting that video. I
acquired nearly three thousand followers just from being in it. At
school, our friends were as freaked out as we were. Every day, someone new walked up to one of us shaking their head in awe and simply
said, "Oh my God." We knew what they meant. Even several teachers
offered congratulations. They followed us, too!

Like Vine itself, this all seemed to happen in six seconds. But we
didn't stop there or rest on the viral success of one video. As is the
case with anyone who gets that kind of reaction, we wanted more. We
wanted to see if we could beat our new record. And so we changed
strategy. We stopped making YouTube videos and concentrated solely
on Vine. We both made at least one new Vine every day. People
looked for them, and between us we added about five hundred new
followers a day.

The next video that went viral was of me jumping into a shopping
cart at the grocery store, holding up a toy sword, and yelling, "For
Narnia!" Logan also made one around that time that took off. By the

start of summer, I had nearly fifteen thousand followers; my brother was closing in on fifty thousand. Both of us kept a close eye on people who were doing similar things to us—people like Jérôme Jarre, Jerry Purpdrank, King Bach, David Lopez, Brittany Furlan, Rudy Mancuso, Marcus Johns, and Nash Grier.

They had millions of followers. They made us laugh. But their Vines didn't seem any different than ours.

"We can do that," I said almost every time I saw one of their Vines.

"I know," my brother agreed. "We just have to keep going."

We realized that climbing the ladder of success, at least as we defined it—more laughs, more likes, more followers, more engagement—hinged on a few things. Doing the work, and making sure our work was good. Those two elements are key to everything: work hard, and do good work. I sound like my dad. Logan and I also realized who we were and the niche we occupied in this crowded world of Viners, and we embraced it. We didn't try to change ourselves or chase the latest trends to try to be more popular. We were the crazy guys who got into shopping carts, jumped into cars with strangers, leaped over families walking down the sidewalk, and, among other things, lip-synched and danced in gym shorts. In a way, it was like high school. The best thing you can possibly do to ensure your popularity is own who you are, and be the best, most genuine version of that. If you're a girl who likes math, solve equations without worrying that guys will think you're nerdy. They won't. They'll think you're a smart girl. If you like drawing or fencing or playing the harmonica, do that. The world of Viners had all the varied personalities of lunchtime in the school cafeteria. Jerry and King Bach were weird, twisted, and off-the-wall funny. Jérôme Jarre was this good-looking, young foreign guy who got away with doing random, silly things by flashing his huge smile. Rudy made Spanish Vines. Brittany Furlan did a female perspective. And Logan and I were the crazy guys who hurt themselves trying to get a laugh.

In June, I went to wrestling camp in Columbus, Ohio, where I put Vine aside to focus on training and competition. I worked hard until one day everyone at camp was showing each other what they were calling the sickest Vine. When one guy showed it to me, I said, "Oh sh*t, that's my brother." Word spread. Guys showed me the video on their phones and said, "No way that's your brother." Then I showed them my Vines, and my followers, which blew them to a whole other realm of disbelief.

"Oh my God," one kid said, "you're Vine famous."

That was the first time I'd been called Vine famous. Not until later that night, as I kicked back following a long, hard day of working out and wrestling, did I think about the idea of having been called Vine famous, about having been recognized for something I'd created, and I thought, *Snap, that is kind of cool.*

It was a motivator. Between workouts, I made a handful of Vines, including one where I dove on a pool table while a couple guys played and I went through the motions of trying to swim. They thought I'd lost my mind; they had no idea I was making a Vine.

"Dude, stop swimming!"

"This is a pool table," I replied, continuing to stroke furiously.

"You're ruining our game."

"But I'll drown if I stop."

"We might have to hurt you worse if you don't."

It was pretty funny, and so was the Vine.

SOME DAYS YOUR UNDERWEAR
STICKS IN YOUR BUTT CRACK.
PICK IT OUT, LAUGH IT OFF, AND GET GOING AGAIN.

SPEAKING OF SWIMMING . . . A SERIOUS CONVERSATION WITH MYSELF

Everyone in high school hits that wall. I'm talking about the question that zooms at you out of nowhere, like a wall you can't help but crash into. That question is this: What am I going to do with my life? Or more simply: What am I going to do?

I hit it about a month after camp. It was July, and I was having fun, making Vines and collecting followers, laughing, acting silly, playing sports and video games, hanging out at Crocker Park, just doing me . . . and then KABOOM! The wall came at me fast and hard, from out of nowhere. Looking back, I can see it was right around the time my brother began preparing to go off to college. He was the spark that lit the fuse.

Logan was excited about leaving home, taking college courses, and making new friends. He was thinking big picture. He dominated the conversations with my parents—and rightfully so. Going to college was a major move for him and for our entire family. Things change, and suddenly I found myself thinking about my future, about how I was going to change, too, and what I was going to do. But before that, I had to ask myself what I *wanted* to do.

What did I want to do?

At age sixteen, such introspective conversations are part of the deal, part of growing up, or of not being grown up yet, and the reality is, the conversations you have with yourself and the questions you ask are difficult. Answers are rarely forthcoming despite wanting them so badly. I tried hard to look into my future, and I saw nothing. Did I want to go to college? My grades were unimpressive. What could I do about that? Or did I want to go with the flow, graduate high school, and eventually go to junior college? What did I want to do? What did I love?

I envied Logan, who was always college-bound and planning on becoming an engineer. Did I want that? Did I want to follow in his footsteps as I had my entire life? Or was there something else for me? And if there was something else, when was I going to find out what it was—and how was I going to know it? Again and again, I asked myself what did I love?

Then I became obsessed with becoming a Navy SEAL. I'd heard about the Navy SEALs from various sources. I watched something about them on YouTube, a movie on TV, and I was blown away by these guys. The SEALs were about everything I loved: cars, guns, trucks, working out, athleticism, physical and mental toughness, and using your brain. Despite my grades, I knew I was smart. I just didn't apply myself. The only thing I put my mind to with the rigor and discipline needed to get better was making Vines, but I didn't see a future in social media yet.

The SEALs inspired in me a vision for the future, something I would work toward becoming. I could see myself as a Navy SEAL. It was exciting. I started reading about the SEALs and studying the requirements. I spoke to an uncle of mine who'd been in the Navy. My dad gave me workouts the SEALs did and played the role of tough drill sergeant—or whatever the Navy SEAL equivalent was—ordering me to jog at top pace for a certain amount of time or hold my breath for two minutes, as SEALs sometimes had to do (I couldn't hold mine that long). We talked about how I'd have to learn to jump from planes and sit in silence for hours. I liked the challenges.

The ultimate challenge came unexpectedly that July, when my dad took my brother, my friend Chance, and me to Chautauqua Lake in western New York. We went there for a week every summer, staying at my dad's best friend's house. It was an awesome place, a mansion on the lake, with a huge yard, dirt bikes, and a dock with a boat we used for fishing and tubing. I always looked forward to going. It was a week of nonstop fun doing all of my favorite things.

One night, after dinner, we were all sitting around a fire pit, and I began talking about being a SEAL. Whenever I brought up the subject, someone—usually my dad or my brother—said something like, "Oh yeah? Can you do 120 push-ups in two minutes?" This time was no different. I had just watched a video on my phone of how SEALs will sit in freezing-cold water for thirty minutes in the middle of the night. All those elements happened to be at hand—a cold night, cold water, and nothing but time to fill. My dad issued the challenge.

"Can you do it?" he said.

"Let's go," I replied.

"No, really," he said.

I was already on my feet.

"I can't turn this down. Let's go do it."

I sprinted to the water as the others ran behind me. At the water's edge, I turned to my dad, my brother, and my friend and gave them a nod that said, "Ready?" Then I jumped into the dark water, fully clothed, and sat there. My brother started the timer on his phone. I sat there motionless, in the freezing water, which was full of algae

and other nasty stuff, whatever it was. I blocked out all the unpleasantness, along with the teasing and taunts from my dad, Logan, and
Chance, who stood six feet away on the shore telling me that I could
quit, that I didn't have to do it, that I'd already proven I was crazy just
by jumping in.

I ignored them. I relaxed my mind and employed the techniques
I'd learned in the book I'd read about Navy SEALs. Pain was mental,
I told myself. The unpleasantness of what I was feeling was only un-
pleasant if I thought about it. The desire to quit was only as strong as
you let it get. It could be trumped by an even stronger desire to succeed. I regulated my breathing. I sent my mind elsewhere.

Then the timer went off.

"That's thirty minutes!" my brother yelled.

"You did it," Chance said.

I walked out of the water cold but triumphant, flashing a satisfied
grin at my dad.

"All right," he said, patting my back. "Let's turn it up a notch."

"What?" I looked at him with disbelief.

"Tomorrow morning, you're swimming across the lake." He grinned.
"That is, if you can do it."

"How long's the lake?" I asked.

"About two miles across," my dad said. "Just what the SEALs have
to swim."

I took a deep breath. I was shivering in the cool night air.

"Okay. Not a problem."

Silence. Just crickets and fireflies.

"I'll do it with you," Chance said.

He also wanted to become a SEAL.

"We're on," I said.

Early the next morning, my dad reminded me of the challenge as

I came downstairs after waking up. I said I was game. So did Chance. We didn't even pause to look across the lake and study the expanse of the two-mile distance we were about to swim. Whatever it was, we were going to conquer it. My dad prepared the boat that he and Logan would pilot alongside us, in case we cramped or quit. I planned to whip up a huge breakfast to power me across the long swim, except I got distracted and forgot to eat. When I heard my dad yelling from the lake—"Okay, let's go! We're ready!"—I grabbed four enormous handfuls of Cheetos, stuffed them into my mouth, and ran out of the house.

It was downhill to the water. I saw my dad and Logan already in the boat, ready to push off the dock. Chance was at the edge of the lake, limbering up. Without stopping or saying a word, I ran past everyone, straight into the water, and began swimming toward the far-off shore on the other side. Chance dove in after me.

The water was cold. I had never been much of a swimmer outside of summer parties with friends, but I had a decent natural stroke, and I was in shape.

Again, I implemented the psychological tactics I'd read about on how to stay strong and focused. Stay in the moment. Take it just four seconds at a time. Imagine being on vacation. Dream while you're awake (a great life tactic, by the way). Take your mind elsewhere. Breathe. Relax. Every time I felt the chill of being in the water, I told myself it was warm and pleasant. Breathe. Relax.

About one-tenth of the way in, Chance stopped swimming and asked to be pulled onto the boat.

"I can't do it," he said. "I'm freezing. I'm tired of swimming. My arms, my legs, everything aches."

I kept going.

The water's warm.

Breathe.

Relax.

Not yet halfway across, I noticed the waves got larger, and they began hitting me in the face. I pushed forward. Then Chance got back in the water. I heard him say something like, "I feel good. If he's doing it, I can do it." A short time later, what I estimated to be slightly more than halfway, my friend waved the white flag again. He climbed back onto the boat, complaining the water was too cold and he was too tired. I kept going. I was in the zone.

Finally, about one hour and fifteen minutes after I ran into the water, I climbed out on the other side of the lake. I literally ran in one end of the lake and walked out the other. I turned toward the boat and raised my fist in a very satisfying sign of triumph.

"I did it!"

In the boat on the way back, my body was completely drained of energy. My arms felt like cold spaghetti. I nearly cramped up, but I was so monstrously happy and pleased with myself. I'd proven something to myself that continues to motivate me to this day and will for the rest of my life: Nothing is impossible. Or to put it another way, anything and everything is possible. If I wanted to be a Navy SEAL later in life, I could do it. If I wanted to be something else, I'd find a way. And I knew I could be successful if I put my mind to it. I knew I could do anything.

But first, there was the rest of the summer. . . .

TODAY WAS AWESOME.

WHY SETTLE FOR ANYTHING LESS?

VINE FAMOUS

After vacation, we went back home and continued making Vines. I made at least one every day. By the middle of summer, the pace, now more predictable and steady, pushed my followers past fifty thousand. Logan was at a hundred thousand. One day, my brother came up with an idea to go into a grocery store in his wrestling singlet, walk up to a stranger, and say, "Let's wrestle!" Obviously, the people he approached didn't want to wrestle, but that didn't stop Logan from daring them to. "Come on, fight me!"

This was the craziest stunt we'd ever done, and the reception proved it. It went viral as soon as we posted it. I got a bunch of followers just from being tagged, but Logan scored in a way that struck us as almost incomprehensible. Not only did he gain a bunch of followers, but they included two of the biggest Viners on the planet, Jérôme Jarre and Marcus Johns. Both commented on his videos, saying basically the same thing: "All of your videos are so funny."

Jérôme actually followed Logan on Twitter, too. When Logan saw that, he followed Jérôme. The next day Jérôme messaged him. *Yo, come to New York and make Vines with me.* My brother and I freaked out. Both of us looked up to Jérôme. He was huge. It was like Lil Wayne DMing me, asking if I wanted to rap with him. I kept saying, "This is insane."

We couldn't stop talking about it the rest of the day. Could he go to New York? Would our parents allow it? What would he do there? Where would he stay? At dinner, we were still talking about the insanity of these guys even knowing who we were, never mind Logan going to New York to make Vines with Jérôme. My mom finally clued in and asked, "What's going on here?"

"Vine is going on," Logan said.

"He's Vine famous," I added.

"So are you," my brother said.

We were cracking up, high-fiving each other. My mom stood there for a long moment, clueless, studying us, trying to understand her sons. Finally she asked the question that was making the rounds of people ten, twenty, and thirty years older than us; in other words, all the people who were just now hearing the buzz about the latest in social media.

"What's Vine?"

Until that point, my parents knew that Logan and I made funny videos. They thought of it as a hobby, like the many sports we played, but without the practices or games. They had no idea of the details or nuances of what we were doing with the videos, how we'd launched Zoosh and then migrated from there to Vine and were emerging as stars. So we sat her down and explained everything about the videos and our followers. Then we did the same with our dad. Both asked, with some amazement, the same questions.

"You have how many followers?"

"What does that mean—that someone is following you?"

"Not someone," I said. "Hundreds of thousands of people are following us."

"Yeah," Logan added, swinging the conversation back to the most urgent matter—Jérôme Jarre. "One of the best and biggest Viners invited me to New York to make Vines with him, and I want to go."

My mom shook her head. She asked more questions, like who

was Jérôme, where did he live, where was Logan going to stay, and all those other mom-type questions. My dad had similar questions. The fact that Logan couldn't answer most of those questions and simply kept repeating they were missing the point, which was that the biggest Viner had invited him to New York to make Vines and he wanted to go, only further convinced them that the most prudent and responsible answer was "no." In fact, they said it repeatedly, resulting in the same conversation over and over:

"No, you can't go."

"Why?"

"We don't think it's the right thing."

"Why?"

"We don't know anything about this Jérôme."

Ultimately, my brother took a stand.

"Fine," he said. "Then I'm not talking to you."

For the next two days, he gave them the silent treatment. My parents caved to a degree. They agreed to gather more information and reconsider their decision, which they did. Logan got more information from Jérôme. He also made a good case for himself, explaining that he'd never gotten into trouble, he was a straight-A student, he'd gotten a full academic scholarship, he'd always abided by their curfews, and, if it came down to it, he was eighteen years old and of legal age to go, regardless of what they said. He said he didn't want to disobey them, but he did want to go super bad.

I stood on the sidelines, watching the drama unfold to what I thought was the inevitable conclusion: My brother was allowed to go. Then extreme envy set in as he went to New York and began making Vines with Jérôme. I had never been to New York or Los Angeles or any major cities. I imagined Manhattan as an enormous, faraway megacity of comic book proportions, where everything was bigger

and more exciting than it was in Cleveland. The texts I got from
Logan documenting his exploits with Jérôme did nothing to dispel
that picture. I saw both him and Jérôme blow up on Vine that week.
A handful of people also texted me about it: "Yo, your brother is with
Jérôme in New York? Making videos? WTF?"

I texted him the same thing.

"WTF?"

He wrote back: "This is insane."

"What do you mean?" I asked.

"I'll explain when I'm back," he said.

By the time he returned home, Logan's followers on Vine had
increased from around two hundred thousand to over five hundred
thousand. This was in the span of a week. Through proximity, my
followers also ballooned past 150,000. It was like picking up overflow
and curiosity seekers. Though I'd continued making Vines daily, Logan's burst of popularity made me feel like I was slacking off. I didn't
like falling behind anyone. Even worse, I was getting lapped. While I
promised myself to close that gap, I was also extremely proud of my
brother. Logan came back a whole new person, motivated, enthusias-
tic, eyes opened to new possibilities, and full of stories.

"Jérôme is a star," he said. "People took pictures of him every-
where we went. Girls. Guys. Tourists. He was constantly recognized.
It was insane."

"Did anyone take a picture of you?" I asked.

"Yeah."

"What the—"

"A couple people knew who I was."

"Ridiculous."

"It was crazy."

It got crazier. Apparently, according to Logan, we could make money from Vine. My eyes grew to the size of basketballs. However it worked, I was in. He'd learned this from Jérôme, who was twenty-five years old: Think like a businessman first and a Viner second, though the two were inextricably linked, and it could be argued creativity had to come first. But as he'd told Logan, he worked to increase his followers with the single-minded purpose of attracting the attention of businesses that paid him to integrate their products in his Vines. His business was being Vine famous. He made money from his six-second antics.

"Cool," I said.

"It's incredible—and totally possible."

It provided a whole new answer to my mom's original question, "What's Vine?" No longer was it just about fun and followers. It was about the potential to make money. For the next month and a half, before Logan left for college, we worked hard at making and posting Vines, and then nurturing shares to increase the followers. Several of mine went viral, including one early favorite, a simple three-beat Wi-Fi joke that began with my brother walking in the front door.

"What's up, dude?" he asked.

"Yo," I said, looking up.

He sat down and took out his phone.

"What's the Wi-Fi?" he asked.

"I don't have Wi-Fi," I said.

"All right," he said, getting up and heading back toward the door. "I'm going to Tom's."

Suddenly I hopped up to 350,000 followers. Logan surpassed 750,000. Social media was popping. Those of us who'd gotten in early and amassed a sizable following had momentum that others entering late couldn't easily catch. If I re-Vined someone, I could get them fifty thousand to a hundred thousand followers and even more views. That was why those of us with followings were being called "influencers," and why companies, at least according to Jérôme, hired people to Vine about their products.

At the end of the summer, before leaving for college, Logan got one of those calls. A company wanted to pay him to make a Vine about their product.

My dad spoke with the company's representative and negotiated a deal that paid my brother $1,000 to make a Vine—the same thing we'd been doing for free to entertain ourselves. That was more than $150 a second (not counting the time spent creating it)—way more than landscaping paid!

Two weeks later, I received an offer from a marketing agent representing a company with a new dating app. I had about four hundred thousand followers now; the numbers were growing weekly. He offered me $250 to make a Vine about the app. I was so eager to get into the game, to get paid, that even though my gut told me I was getting ripped off, or at least charging way too little, I emailed back, "Okay, let's do it."

One day, as I thought about ways I could grow my followers, I reached out to Max Jr, a Vine superstar from Los Angeles whose work I admired. We followed each other; then I got his phone number and, via a text, asked if he could video himself saying a line that I wrote so I could incorporate it into one of my Vines. He did, and that became my first ever collab.

Then, without me having to ask, Max Jr shared my Vine for about thirty minutes on his profile, which introduced me to his million-plus followers, some of whom liked me, and incredibly, I started eleventh grade with more than five hundred thousand followers. I was growing my Twitter, too. I was popular beyond any expectation I'd ever had, and I had the data as proof. It was a high school fantasy come true. I thought I was going to have the best year of my life.

I couldn't have been more wrong.

WAKE UP. NO, REALLY. WAKE UP!

NOW, GO DO IT.

HATERS

Whether you're in your teens or twenties, popularity is an issue. The idea of being liked is important. Belonging to the right or cool group is also important. I wish it weren't like that. Too much is made of who is in and who is not. It's a stupid, artificial fact of junior high and high school that shouldn't inhibit you from friendships of any sort. I'm all about breaking down those barriers, talking to anyone who interests you, and not worrying about whether it's cool.

I began eleventh grade having a helluva good time. I was getting better at making videos and also at understanding everything related to what made a video successful: the mechanics of social media, marketing, and my audience. I grew my YouTube and Twitter presences. Then, thanks to a girl I met via social media, I got turned on to Instagram. She was visiting Cleveland from Indiana and told me she had the most followers on Instagram of anyone in her home state.

"It's easy," she said. "Everyone's gonna be on it."

"Okay, I'll try it and see what happens," I said.

I created an Instagram account and then I made a Vine telling people to follow me on Instagram. Within twenty-four hours, I got thirty-five thousand followers. This kind of cross-platform success only made me try harder, and I kept doing my thing. Offers for money came in a little more frequently, and at increasingly larger sums, too. I went from $250 for a Vine to $600, $750, and then $1,000. I wish I could say I did something brilliant with the money. But as soon as the checks cleared, I went to the mall and bought stuff. I had a new iPhone, a fancy watch, and nine pairs of Nike LeBrons, all in different colors.

I didn't play football that year. For the first time in my life, I sat out a season, because the game stopped being fun. I went to the games as a spectator instead. Though it was a different experience, I still enjoyed supporting my school and hanging out with friends. Then something strange happened. I began to get recognized. At game after game, kids came up and asked to take a picture with me. It happened at Friday night basketball games, too. At one event, twenty to thirty kids all came up at once. I saw the adults around me wondering who I was and overheard a kid say to his parent, "He makes Vines. He's famous."

I did wrestle. When the season started, I threw myself into practices and matches, winning some tough early matches that made me feel positive about the season, and school felt pretty much as it always had, until something happened that confounds me to this very day. It was right around the time I passed 750,000 followers on Vine. Suddenly and inexplicably, my popularity at school plummeted. I don't know why it happened, whether it was jealousy or anger at my success, or whether I came off as a braggart, which wasn't who I was or am. It doesn't matter; it happened—and it hurt.

The first time I remember was at a Friday night basketball game. I was in the stands with a couple friends, and instead of coming up to me for photos, classmates stared at me, pointed, and whispered cruel comments that were easily overheard. "He thinks he's so cool. But he's really cocky. Everybody hates him." At Crocker Park, kids got right in my face. "Your brother is so much better—at everything." And: "Your Vines suck."

I ignored them as best I could and instead tried to understand the thinking behind the collective shift. From what I figured out, there were about fifty kids that turned on me. They were mostly the popular kids, some of whom I had been in class with and played alongside on teams, and I think they simply hated my popularity.

For whatever reason, they were haters. I was targeted in nasty tweets on an almost daily basis, and many of those were retweeted. The strange part was, these involved people who'd previously said, "Good videos," "What up, bro?," or "Good game." Before one wrestling match, I walked in for my warm-up and the gym went completely silent, as if on cue. Later in the season, someone put up a Vine showing me getting beat in the final of a tournament and saying I was a wimp and a loser.

You wouldn't think a top wrestler and former football player like me would be vulnerable to such things, but my feelings were like anyone else's, especially one day when a kid's tweet about me got four hundred fifty favorites. That was like one hundred times more favorites than a typical tweet would get. It was like the whole school started to go against me.

I handled things fairly well, at least I think so, until someone insulted my mom on Twitter. My natural inclination was to go looking for the SOB who said those things, but I knew that wasn't the right way to deal with the situation, so I sat and stewed about what to do, and instead found myself turning all the negative tweets and Vines into a collage that I put on my phone.

Eventually my mom came into the kitchen, asked what I was doing, glanced at my phone, and then was stunned when she saw what I can only describe as a billboard of hate. She recognized some of the kids; she was even friendly with a few of their moms. She had no idea the extent this hatred had spread.

"How long has this been going on?" she asked.

"Awhile," I said, with reluctance, not wanting to answer any questions but nonetheless giving her enough information to call the school's principal and rip him a new one.

I hadn't seen my mom that angry, *ever*.

Still, at nearly six feet tall and able to physically take care of myself on the football field or wrestling mat, I didn't want my mom fighting my battles. But I have to admit, I did sit back and admire her fiery willingness to take on the school's ultimate authority, and when she finally hung up the phone, I asked for a recap.

"He said he wasn't aware this was going on," she said. "I don't see how he can run a school and not be aware that hundreds of kids are seeing and 'liking'"—she made quotation marks—"these hate-filled Twitters."

"Tweets."

She looked at me like I didn't get it, which I didn't—until she explained.

"Jake, here's what I want you to do," she said. "Ignore everything. Ignore them. Concentrate on all the good things you have going for you."

"You're right," I said. "It's dumb of me to feed into it."

It wasn't easy, but I took my mom's advice to heart and from then on I separated myself from the haters. I ignored them at school and ignored them on social media. *Let 'em hate,* I thought. *What a waste of their time and energy.* Instead, I applied myself to the activities that made me happiest—working out, boxing, doing MMA, and of course making Vines, which continued to get better and gain me more followers. So I had fewer friends at school, but a growing chorus of fans across the country and around the world. It was a lesson in believing in myself, and having the last laugh—and I did!

Around that time, in January, shortly after school had resumed following the Christmas holiday, I got an email. It was the best email I'd ever opened, and though I no longer have the original, the email was like this: "Hey Jake I am Thanh Nguyen, and I am promoting a tour that's going to be in Houston and Dallas." At that point, I was already in. I didn't need to read any more. But it got better. "I'd like you to participate. We'll fly you down, put you up in a hotel, and give you $1,000 to be there and meet fans."

According to the email, some of the hottest Vine stars were already signed up, including Jerry Purpdrank, Max Jr, and YouTube OG Sam Pottorff, which was amazing. But another participant captured my attention equally: "Miss Teen Texas." I didn't know who she was—and it didn't matter. I read "Miss Teen Texas," and I went from "I'm in" to "Nothing is going to keep me from going."

I took the proposal to my dad and asked if I could go. He raised a skeptical eyebrow, as he did in such circumstances, and he asked me a ton of questions. Who's the guy that contacted you? What do you know about him? What are the dates? Who's paying for the plane ticket? What hotels are they putting you up in? Is there a contract? Do you know when you get paid? How you get paid?

They were all the questions a responsible parent should ask, but I didn't have all the answers—not yet, anyway. Neither did I need them. I was ready to get on a plane right then. I could stay home and go to school, which was a miserable experience. Or I could fly to Texas for four days and get paid a lot of money to hang out with fans.

My dad understood. He spoke with Thanh Nguyen, who provided all the details, which sounded legit, and then came into my room to give me the news: "All right, you can go." As I celebrated, I realized something that suddenly made the trip even sweeter. The tour was going to coincide with my birthday, on January 17.

"Sick!" I said to myself. "I'm going to be on tour on my birthday, with some of my favorite Viners *and* Miss Teen Texas."

It was already the best birthday present of my life.

    •   •   •

NOTE: This was a tough chapter to read. But it had a happy ending.

☺

I can do a better happy face than that.

HAPPY FACE

STOP READING FOR A MINUTE
AND LIKE ME.
MORE IMPORTANT, *LIKE* YOURSELF!

THE MOST FUN NIGHT I EVER HAD (AND THAT WAS BEFORE I MET MISS TEEN TEXAS IN PERSON)

Admittedly, my reputation as a player with the ladies was deserved. It was always in fun, and nothing serious ever developed. The girls I hung out with turned into good friends. Even after a flirtation ended, we still hung out with the group at Crocker Park. If a former fling needed a ride home, I never hesitated to offer the passenger seat in my Jeep. I enjoyed looking and playing without any ties. I never got to where I was "talking" with one particular girl. There was never that one special person that I had feelings for—until I met Kellie Stewart.

From the time I read that Miss Teen Texas was going to be on the Infiniti tour, as it was called, I had a sense that something might happen between us. That was wishful thinking, of course, but WTF, I seemed to be living one dream, why not start creating another dream come true? I found pictures of her on the Internet—not a difficult thing to do. When someone has won a beauty pageant, they're pretty much photographed a gazillion times.

I messaged her.

"Yo, we are going to be on tour together. How awesome is that?"

Yeah, that was a little bold, but I had confidence with girls.

Also, if you want something, you have to risk failure. Kellie was tall and blond and beautiful. There was nothing un-awesome about her or about the idea of hanging out together for the four days of the tour.

She reciprocated by sending me her number. I texted her until the tour started. I was beyond excited to get there. Though this was my first trip anywhere alone, my parents were cool. I didn't get any lectures or instructions. They knew I was prepared. I didn't smoke or do drugs. I was a good kid with an abundance of energy and curiosity and this weird and growing success in social media, which they supported now that they understood it better. Letting me go was the right thing to do.

When we got to the airport, I realized this was the first time I would be flying by myself. I enjoyed every moment. From takeoff to landing, my face was pressed against the window. I loved looking at the ground from high above. My head was filled with ideas for videos. I thought about Kellie. Several times I laughed out loud. People turned to look at me, but for all the right reasons. I was having the best time of my life, and I hadn't even arrived yet.

Once I was on the ground in Houston, Thanh picked me up outside the terminal. He already had Sam Pottorff in the car. Sam had just arrived from Los Angeles. I was excited to meet this OG YouTuber. As Thanh drove through Houston, I stared out the window in awe of the sleek glass high-rise buildings that cluttered the city's skyline. Cleveland had a downtown area, but not like Houston's. I'd never seen anything like it.

"Anyone want to stop at Whataburger?" Thanh asked.

Sam immediately said he was in—maybe for two, plus fries.

I was silent. I didn't know what to say.

"Have you ever been to a Whataburger?" Thanh asked.

"No, what is it?" I said.

"Dude, it's the best hamburger ever!"

"All right." I smiled. "Let's go."

An hour later, I was full and texting friends back home that I'd just eaten the best burger of my life. It was a really cool way to start the trip—with an awesome burger, meeting Sam, and hearing about Los Angeles. Sam was the first person I had met from L.A., and I peppered him nonstop with questions about everything: the ocean, the sun, the stars, the scene, Hollywood—even the HOLLYWOOD sign up in the hills that I'd seen on TV and in magazines.

"It sounds amazing," I said. "I really want to get out there."

"You need to," he said, nodding.

We rolled up in front of the hotel, and I couldn't believe the sight in front of my eyes: Dozens of fans were waiting outside, hoping to catch sight of us even before the tour. As we got out of the car, they screamed and yelled our names. Again, I was blown away by the two separate worlds I inhabited, one with haters and this one, with girls screaming for Sam and me. It was like a dream, except it was real.

I followed the guys to the front desk and checked in. The guy there found my name and asked how many room keys I wanted.

"What?"

"How many keys would you like us to make for you?"

"It's just me. So one, I guess."

"All right."

He handed me the key. In the elevator, I thought, *Oh my God, I have a hotel room by myself. This is crazy.* Once settled, I texted Kellic.[19]

"Yo, are you coming?"

---

19 Again, I don't have the original texts, but I re-created the conversation as best as possible.

She responded within seconds.

"Oh, they canceled me last-minute."

"Damn."

"Are you going to the Dallas event?" she asked.

"Yeah, the day after tomorrow. We're driving down from here."

"I live only thirty minutes from where you'll be," she wrote.

"Great. Maybe we can meet up. I really want to meet you."

I hadn't been able to stop thinking about her. She was the hottest girl I'd ever seen and she was famous. Verified on Twitter.

"Okay, see you there."

I explored my hotel room, checking out the bathroom, the closet, and the remote control for the large flat-screen TV; it wasn't the most luxurious hotel room ever, but it was mine, and being there made me feel strangely, newly, wonderfully independent.

I turned on the TV and scrolled through the dozens of HD channels until it was time to meet Sam and Thanh for dinner. I had a hard time believing this was my life when Sam and Thanh showed up with Jerry Purpdrank and Max Jr. These guys were superstars, my heroes, and here they were—and they knew who I was!

I'd done a collab, of course, with Max Jr, but we'd never met in person or even spoken; everything had been via text and email. Now I wasn't just meeting him and the other guys, I was one of them. Amazing!

We talked the entire night about social media. Little things that non-pros don't think about, like the strategies of posting, ideas, fans, how to grow your followers, tricks we use to get more followers, techniques we developed for making videos, how much to charge corporations for posts, and the future of different social-media platforms. Tons of stuff. Then it got interesting.

"After this, me and Jerry are flying to L.A.," Max Jr said. "We're going to meet with a bunch of people to see if we can make something out of it."

"Good idea," Sam said. "I live there. I have a manager."

"What's a manager?" I asked.

I was clueless.

"Maybe we can get acting jobs, TV and all that stuff," Jerry said.

"You totally can," Sam said.

I stared at him, transfixed. I tried to imagine Los Angeles: actors, managers, agents, and the HOLLYWOOD sign in the hills. The thing was, I couldn't imagine it. I had no points of reference. I asked more questions. Should I have an agent? How much money do you make once you have several million followers?

I wanted to know everything, and there was so much to know. With my brother at college, I hadn't been able to talk with anyone about Vine and social media for nearly five months. It was like meeting fellow aliens from the same planet, in the middle of Texas.

"Check out this Louis Vuitton bracelet and these Vuitton shoes," Sam said.

My eyes were as large as Rolex watches. I'd never seen anyone back home with Vuitton gear. I fired another question at Sam.

"Have you ever seen a Lamborghini? Because I haven't, not in real life."

"Dude, I see a Lamborghini every single day," he said.

Time flew by that night. I finally went back to my room. The next morning I woke up and went straight to the event. There, my sole responsibility was to meet fans. I'd never done anything remotely like this and I had no idea what to expect—until we pulled up in front of the venue and saw what the promoter estimated was more than six hundred people waiting outside. Just as they had at the hotel the previous day, the crowd, mostly girls, screamed our names as soon as they saw us get out of the car and head inside.

Despite being hurried into the enormous conference room for the event, I stopped and took a video of the craziness rippling through the crowd of people. I zoomed in on a girl wearing a shirt with my picture on the front. I sent the video to my parents, my friends, and my brother.

"Insane!" a friend messaged me. "What's going on there?"

Logan wrote back: "Dude, are you serious?"

The day was a nonstop line of meeting fans, posing for pictures, and signing my name on T-shirts, arms, pictures, and other souvenirs people brought. My fans were so cool. I enjoyed every second of the time I spent meeting them; what a cool thing, to be able to make a personal connection with people who had bought tickets and waited in line because they liked me. All the posts on Twitter and Instagram made it feel like we took over social media. I wondered if the event trended that day. I never had the chance to check.

After the event, Thanh took us all out to a nice restaurant for dinner. Before we ordered, he handed each of us an envelope, our payment for doing the tour. Mine contained $1,000 in cash. Ten crisp $100 bills. I'd never seen that large a sum in cash. It seemed like a fortune. The money put everybody in an even better mood, and dinner turned into a loud, fun birthday celebration for me. At some point during the evening, I checked my phone and saw Logan had messaged me. At the time, I had 950,000 followers on Vine, and he'd posted a Vine to his 1.5 million followers: "Hey, my brother's b-day is tomorrow. Let's give him a present and get him to one million followers."

Back at the hotel, I checked my Vine account and let loose with a big whoo-hoo! Thanks to my brother, I'd passed one million followers.

Then, a couple minutes later, it was officially my birthday, and all of a sudden my phone lit up with messages. The first one was the best. It was from Logan: "Happy birthday, bro."

A MISS TEEN TEXAS DREAM COMES TRUE

Early the next morning, I got into a car with Jerry and Max and we began the drive to Dallas. All of us looked like we'd just woken up, and we had. I was still exhausted, and about an hour into the drive I fell asleep in the backseat. When I woke up, my head was in that halfway place between sleep and awake, where I was trying to make sense of my life at that moment: I was in the backseat of a car, heading to Dallas with two of the biggest social-media stars in the world, both of whom had helped me celebrate my birthday the night before. It seemed more dreamlike than real; I never wanted to wake up from this feeling.

A song by Soulja Boy and Drake came on the radio, and I heard them rapping, "We made it." It was a magical, exhilarating instance of life and the universe all seeming perfectly in sync with the music. Everything just felt right and good, to the point where, as I lay in the backseat, I became one with everything about that song, from the beat to the story the lyrics told, how they had finally made it after a lifetime of no one caring about their dreams or believing they could actually achieve them. They were describing the way I felt just then, and I was so into it.

By the end of the song, I was fully awake and sitting up, looking out the window at the towering Dallas skyline in the distance. I'd never seen a city like the one ahead of us or experienced anything like this tour. I was with my idols. I'd just turned seventeen. I was meeting fans. I was having so much fun.

And then, of course, I was texting Kellie, asking if she would show up and just say hi.

"What are you doing, bro?" one of the guys asked.

"Texting Kellie."

"Who?"

"Miss Teen Texas."

They laughed, as did I, except I was in on the joke. Less than a year earlier I had asked myself what I wanted to do with my life, and now I knew. Not only that, I was headed in the right direction. Though I hadn't made it yet, I was confident I would eventually get there—not by taking the traditional route of high school, college, and more schooling. It was going to be a different path, one that I'd been on for a long time whether I knew it or not. I was living and loving this thing I'd created, and I couldn't think of anything else . . . well, almost anything else. There was still Miss Teen Texas.

I checked my phone. No messages from Kellie.

Frustrating.

Anyway.

We did the event, which lasted the rest of the day. The Dallas crowd was just like Houston's, only more people showed up. Jerry and Max saw me checking my phone for word from Kellie. I kept shaking my head.

"She's not going to come," I said, disappointment clouding my face.

"Don't worry about it," Max told me.

"There are plenty of girls," Sam added. "Wait till you get to L.A. Your eyes are going to explode."

Longboarding on a cold, cloudy day in Santa Monica.

LEFT: All dressed up and looking cute at my mom's wedding.
ABOVE: A family camping trip with my dad and brother in Colorado.

Before Homecoming my freshman year. (Damn, I was awkward.)

Someone's a little fishy.

Marcus, me, and Lucas—victims of a gang fight with Smurfs.

With A.J. in Newport Beach, feeling the summer vibes.

Chillin', front row, at the J. Cole concert in L.A.

Cotton-candy-mouthed with
Alissa Violet at the Santa Monica Pier.

Surfing with Neels in his hometown,
Newport Beach.

With Alex, Lucas, Marcus, and Neels at the Air + Style snowboarding event.

I fell right after this picture was taken and everyone landed on me. But that's cool—you're supposed to help your friends.

Downtown L.A.—under a bridge—celebrating . . .

We did this so many times to get
it perfect that we drew a crowd.

With Neels,
trying to look artsy and edgy.

Nothing can stop us, we're all the way up . . .

Don't try this at home. But if you're in Beverly Hills, go for it.

Uh . . . shirts are overrated.

They kept talking about Los Angeles until I was about to ask if we could skip the Dallas event and go straight to the airport for the next flight to L.A. But the Dallas event was equally fun and exciting as the one in Houston, with one difference. As we entered the final part of the event, the exclusive meet-and-greet for VIP ticket holders, I got a text from Kellie. "Hey, we are twenty minutes away." I freaked out.

"Dude, what's going on?" Max asked.

"She's on her way."

The next twenty minutes of autographs, photos, and conversation with fans happened in a blur. I was unable to concentrate as I waited for her to arrive.

Then it happened: Toward the end of the VIP meet-and-greet, she got there, and as she walked in, accompanied by a girlfriend, it seemed like every head in the place turned in her direction, including mine. My eyes followed her as she searched the crowd until she spotted me, made eye contact, waved, and walked toward me. I had one thought: *Oh my God, she's perfect from head to toe.*

Up close, she was even more beautiful. I'd never seen a girl that pretty. It threw me off my game, which had never happened before. She noticed the way fans were going crazy over me and I could see she was impressed. Jerry and Max were wingman-ing me, which was one of the coolest things in my life ever. They talked me up and gave her the lowdown on why these people were excited to meet me.

Kellie took it all in until the event finished, which wasn't long. Then Jerry, Max, and I made small talk with Kellie and her friend. We didn't have any plans for the remainder of the night; I wanted to make some, but didn't have the guts to suggest anything. I'd put all my energy into hoping Kellie would simply make it to the event.

"When are you going back home?" she asked.

"Tomorrow morning," I said.

Awkward silence.

"So are the two of you taking off now?" I asked.

"No." Kellie smiled. "We're going to show you around Dallas."

Huge grins.

"Awesome."

Max had to do something else and peeled off in another direction, but Jerry stuck with us as we walked outside and into the parking lot. Kellie led us to a sick-looking convertible BMW, her prize for winning the state's beauty pageant. Soon we were cruising through Dallas, with the world's most beautiful tour guide pointing out the sights. There was lots of conversation and laughter. We cracked jokes and found out things we had in common. It was clear we were hitting it off, especially Kellie and me.

"Anyone feel like a milk shake?" she asked.

Everyone shouted yes, and Kellie took us to a cool ice-cream place. She and I shared a milk shake, and we spent the rest of the evening flirting with each other. Afterward, we made a bunch of Vines, and finally it got late enough where Kellie and her friend said they had to go. She drove us back to the hotel, where Jerry and Kellie's friend got out of the car, so Kellie and I had a moment to ourselves to say goodbye.

We sat in awkward silence for a few seconds. We stared at each other, then looked away, fidgeted, then looked back at each other. Finally, she smiled and broke the silence:

"Well, bye."

"Bye," I said. "I'll come back and visit you."

"That would be great." She smiled.

We kept sitting there. It was obvious we liked each other but weren't ready to express that sentiment, not that it's anything you typically say on the first date. Thus the long patch of silences. Finally, it was time to go. She had to get home, and nothing else was going to be accomplished by sitting there. I leaned forward and gave her a hug goodbye. She hugged me back, and I got out of the car, feeling stoked about her and the night and everything as I watched her drive off.

Later that night, Kellie texted me: "I really like you. You're awesome." I replied with a similar message and got a response—though not the one I expected—seconds later: "There's just one problem. I'm kind of talking to this other guy." I was like, "Oh? Whatever." I didn't care. "I'm going to text you anyway." Her reply was short and sweet. ":)"

APPRECIATE WHAT YOU HAVE.

BEFORE IT TURNS INTO WHAT YOU HAD.

ÇA NE VA PAS DURER ÉTERNELLEMENT

Back in Ohio, I returned to normal life: attending school and wrestling. But I couldn't help wonder if this was still normal life. Did I even have a normal life anymore? Did I have to even think in terms of normal? Why limit myself? I had experienced a different kind of life, one that was extraordinary, exciting, and fun, and filled with opportunities and possibilities, interesting, talented people, and one very hot—no, make that *super* hot—girl. Just one of those things can make your head spin. I had all of them. So why was I going to boring classes and dealing with haters?

The haters returned. After seeing Kellie and me together on Vine and Instagram, they spread the word I was stuck-up. I wasn't. I didn't boast. I just lived my life. One day, about a month after the tour, Kellie FaceTimed me. She looked great, and I told her so. But I could see something was up. She had a look in her eye; I could tell she was emotional and wanted to talk. Finally, I got right to it.

"Did you and that guy stop talking?"

She nodded. "Yeah."

She's incredible, I thought. I couldn't believe she had needed to break this news to *me*!

"I'm sorry to hear that," I said.

She looked straight at me with big eyes overflowing with emotion; she appeared serious and vulnerable. I said something funny and sweet, and the corners of her mouth turned upward, into the start of a smile—and the start of our relationship. From then on, we began texting and talking daily.

This was an altogether new experience for me. She was the first girl I'd ever cared about in an emotional way, and I had to get used to the strange way that made me feel, though I can't say I was ever successful. It was like being hungry all the time, without having any food nearby, and the fact Kellie lived in another state didn't help.

We talked as often as possible, and Kellie was a sympathetic listener when I vented about missing out on exciting career opportunities. As an up-and-coming model herself, who also was in school, she understood my frustration, like why it was torture when my friends from the tour, Jerry and Max, called and said Beats By Dre had paid them a bunch of money to make Vines.

To me, it wasn't only about the money. Every day I walked into a classroom I had the sense I was wasting precious time, that I wasn't doing what I was supposed to be doing with my life, what I was most passionate about, what made me feel 100 percent me. This was driven home one day in French class. I was having trouble concentrating in school in general, and French class challenged me in the worst way. I couldn't understand why I was there. Even when I was there, part of me was elsewhere.

One day the teacher, Mme Baker, called on me, and as was typically the case, I wasn't paying attention. I didn't hear her ask a question. I didn't even see her standing in front of my desk—and then it was too late.

"Monsieur Paul?"

I heard her knocking but I wasn't ready to let her in.

I'd been Vining a lot. Several major companies had contracted me to make Vines for an increasing amount of money. I got $5,000 for one project, double that for another, and even more for a third. So it wasn't for nothing that my mind was focused on Vine ideas rather than on conjugating French verbs.

Mme Baker didn't care, and she let me know it.

"*Ça ne va pas durer éternellement*, Monsieur Paul," she said.

"Huh?" I replied, startled. "I don't know what you said."

"I know you don't." She glared.

"Sorry. What's up?"

"*Écoutez!*"

"Okay."

"I said, 'Your Vines—it's not going to last forever.' "

What the? Suddenly she had my complete attention, and then some. *It's not going to last forever.* Those words echoed in my brain. I stared straight at her, with an expression that conveyed the intense anger her ignorance had ignited in me; she stared back. We were communicating with each other better than any time previously—not in French, not in English, not even with words. Then, in a way I don't really have the ability to describe, I blinked and she disappeared from my life. Oh, she was still next to me, and in fact she was speaking to me, and even speaking about me, as she stepped back in front of the classroom, trying to make an example of me to my classmates—her way of regaining authority. I didn't care. I was finished with her, and the class.

I turned my head and looked out the window, and beyond—all the way to Los Angeles, where I swear I saw a massive party going on in the offices of Beats By Dre.

The bell rang—and I heard that.

I got up from my desk and headed for the door, speaking the last few words of French I would ever say.

"Au re-f*#king-voir." [20]

I was done with French—and with school. Not with learning, though. No way was I finished with learning. But I was so over school when I walked out the door that day. My classmates had turned against me and my teachers were unsupportive. I arrived home steaming with resentment. I opened the fridge, slammed a bottle of milk onto the counter, and chowed down on whatever I could reach. Ordinarily, I have always been a pretty even-tempered guy. I don't get angry. I leave that to other people; it's such a waste of time and energy. But this was an exception. My mom saw it immediately, and she didn't have to ask what happened before I told her.

"I can't believe my teacher said that to me!" I railed.

"She was trying to help, I'm sure she was trying to help," my mom said.

"Mom, why am I in school? What does that teacher know? Why am I wasting time in her class? What is she going to teach me?"

The questions poured out of me.

"Why do I need to stay in school? Why do I need to go to college? Why am I not out in Los Angeles with guys like Jerry and Max and—"

"How old are those guys?" she asked.

"In their twenties," I said.

"That's why they're in Los Angeles and you're here in Cleveland. They're of age; you are still—"

"But I have more than a million followers."

"And think of how much more they'll like you when you finish college."

---

20 Pardon my French.

I couldn't think of anything other than not going to school any-more and being in Los Angeles, where I could pursue opportunities as a Viner. I wanted to be back in the car with Jerry and Max, feeling like I did when we were outside of Dallas, feeling like I was on my way, feeling like that song "We Made It" was speaking to me. Instead I felt stuck in the mud. I had a few other outbursts ("No, I'm not going to get good grades," and so on) in front of my dad, who nodded and was like, "Whatever." He treated my frustration the way he did when he coached me in football. He let me burn it off. Though I'm surprised he didn't make me do push-ups. In retrospect, he probably should've. You can't change everything to be the way you want it. Sometimes, you have to do things you don't want to do to get where you want to go. As I have come to say, the grind never ends.

This particular grind was tough. Life was changing and I was changing, and I could see and feel it. Yet I had so little power to do anything. Welcome to being a teenager—I know. But it was an in-tense time of waking up. It was a little like my video where I jumped out of a bush in front of a crowd of people in a crosswalk saying, "It worked! It worked! What year is this?" I didn't know where I was. I think every teenager has that period when they look around at their life and ask, "Where am I?" I felt it strongest one week when I went to a wrestling tournament. I loved wrestling. I was good at it—better than good. But once at this tournament, I went through a severe about-face. I stood in the middle of the gym, looked around at the stands, looked up at the lights high in the ceiling, and asked, "What does it matter?"

Not the best thing to have in your head before squaring off on the mat against guys wanting to throw you down so hard you can't get up. That didn't happen, thankfully. But I did put myself in a men-tal chokehold. "This is one tournament in all of America," I said to myself, "in this one city. In this random gym. In this random school. Which no one cares about. I mean, who cares? There are three other divisions, fourteen other weight classes, and people competing in all fifty states. . . . Unless I'm a national champion, which I'm not, what does it mean? What does it matter?"

What I came to realize is, it does matter. I can't describe all the ways it matters, because I'm still only nineteen and figuring things out. But, looking back, the thing that mattered most is that I didn't quit. I didn't quit wrestling right then. In fact, I went on to have a pretty good tournament and a pretty decent season. I forced myself to grind it out. I got some backbone from it. The adults in my life used words like *perseverance* and *fortitude*. I like the word *grind*— sometimes it's more like *griiiiiiind*. My brother talks about feeling the burn. The burn is good. It's where you want to get to. You feel it when you push yourself to do more than you did before, or, as in this case of me and school, when you push yourself to do something you don't want to but have to do.

But *c'est la vie*.

Oh shoot, there I go speaking French again.

JAKE PAUL HATES IT WHEN YOU TOUCH HIS BELLY BUTTON

There might be a very tiny bit of mystery around the question of why Kellie Stewart once posted a Vine that said, "Jake Paul hates it when you touch his belly button." Maybe there's not any mystery. Maybe people don't care. Certainly there's no mystery around why Kellie posted the Vine. However, in case someone has spent the past few years wondering why the very beautiful former Miss Teen Texas revealed that about me, I will attempt to clear things up.[21]

We got together over spring break. Miserable in school, especially after wrestling season ended, I was counting the days until the end of the school year in June, when suddenly, April snuck up on me, and with it, a week of vacation (bookended by two weekends). Nine full days of no school, no haters, no nothing but time to make Vines. I was also texting with Kellie, who was the first to ask what I was doing over break. Within minutes, I asked my parents if I could go to Texas.

"I can fly there," I said. "I will pay for it with my money."

"Where are you going to stay?"

---

21 Even if there's only one person out there wondering about my touch-sensitive belly button, I'm going to explain.

"At Kellie's."

"Do her parents know?"

"I'm sure they'll be cool with it."

As it turned out, they were cool with it. Our parents spoke beforehand, assuring each other that each of them was raising a good, normal kid, if you can call a beauty queen and a professional Viner normal teenagers. Though we hadn't seen each other since January, when I was last in Texas, we'd texted multiple times daily and considered ourselves to be "talking," which was more committed than I'd ever been with a girl. Then again, she wasn't just any ordinary girl, not with that long blond hair, sculpted features, and sparkle in her eye. I was so nervous about seeing her in person again that I left my suitcase in Cleveland.

"Really?" she asked, laughing.

"I didn't think I needed anything more than my smile," I said.

Not really, I was way too nervous to say anything that smooth. As I said, the fact that this girl stood five foot ten and was prettier than any model I'd seen in magazines threw me off my game. I also cared about her in a weird way I didn't know how to deal with, since it was the first time that had happened. Plus, despite all the texting and talking we'd done the past few months, it was awkward seeing her in person. Right there, three inches away from me, so close I could've kissed her if I'd had the nerve, which I didn't—not then.

We got into her BMW and drove around Dallas. She showed me a bunch of places where she hung out. The city was so modern and big, compared to Cleveland. I looked right and left, up and down, but mostly at her. She drove to a nice restaurant, where there was a prime parking spot waiting just for us. She pulled in and turned off the engine. Neither of us made a move to open the door. She turned toward me; I was already looking at her. Our eyes locked, and in that instant all the awkwardness of knowing we liked each other but not being comfortable being ourselves melted away and we leaned forward and kissed. It was great. And so was dinner.

Afterward, we went to her house. I met her parents. Her dad lectured me about not sneaking out of my room, treating her right, and all that stuff, to which I responded, "Yes sir, for sure. I'm a good kid." And I was—and so was she. For the next four days, we hung out at her house, splashed in the hot tub, swam, went to the mall, talked, and had fun. We got along really well.

A while later, she visited me in Ohio. I

FIRST-KISS DOS & DON'TS

Do: Communicate. It would've been less awkward if I'd texted Kellie, "Do you want to kiss tonight when I see you?"
Don't: Be scared.

Do: Make a joke if you're nervous. When it was quiet between Kellie and me, but we knew we liked each other and we knew it was going to happen, I could've said, "This isn't awkward at all."
Don't: Pretend it's not your first kiss.

Do: Be confident. Be like, "Yo, you know what would be cool right now? If we kissed."
Don't: Worry. You wouldn't be in this spot if it wasn't going to happen.

Do: Say, "That was great. I like you a lot."
Don't: Say, "Do you want a breath mint?"

realized you know you like someone when you can spend time with them without worrying about being anything but yourself. I showed her around my hometown, introduced her to a few of my friends, went to Crocker Park, saw a movie, got smoothies, and all that stuff. The best times, though, were those spent at my house, not doing anything other than laughing, acting silly, and making Vines, including one where she asked me to dance.

"Jake, Jake, dance with me," she said.

As we started to dance, she reached toward me and tweaked my belly button. It was a trick! As she'd learned earlier, I'm so ticklish in that particular spot that if someone touches me there, I scream. Incredibly loud. WHOAOAHAHAHAHAAAAA! I can't help it. I've seen specialists from around the world for this condition, and the diagnosis is unanimous. I'm freakin' ticklish. The prescription? Don't touch Jake Paul's belly button. Why? Because Jake Paul hates it when you touch his belly button.[22]

Hey, everyone has a weakness.

•   •   •

There was a strange moment when I took Kellie to the airport. I think it stemmed from both of us being focused on pursuing careers outside of school, especially me. As Kellie knew, I wanted to go after social media 100 percent and see where it took me. She wanted to model, and I wanted out of school, out of Ohio, and into a whole new life. We talked a lot about it, and so right before she got on her flight, she must've sensed we were destined to move in different directions, because she said, "I hope this isn't the last time I see you."

"Hopefully not," I said, really meaning it.

After that, I don't know, it was different between us. As predicted, I became more focused on my career, and it was hard to maintain a long-distance relationship. But I hope I meant half as much to her as she does to me. Kellie will always be the first girl who really touched my heart—and my belly button.

WHOAOAHAHAHAHAAAAA!

---

22 Of course, if you're an amazing blonde, touch away. Just know that I'm going to scream like a little girl.

FIRST-DATE TUTORIAL

Everyone has first-date anxiety. It comes from a mix of anticipation, excitement, and the unknown. I have an analogy—jumping into a cold swimming pool. You know how you stand on the side for about ten minutes, debating whether to go in? You dip your toe in. You look around. You brace yourself for that first instant of shock, from comfortable to freezing. You tell yourself you're going to do it anyway. You count to three. Then you change your mind and count to ten or seventeen or whatever. Finally, you go, "What the F, I'm hot and want to swim," and you jump. That's a first date. It doesn't require anything more than accepting the fact that you want to swim and realizing everyone else also has first-plunge jitters.

The part about first dates that you should put energy into is planning what you will do on them. I have some tips; they start with what you shouldn't do. Don't go out to eat. I know, it's the first thing you think of and everyone seems to do it. But I'm telling you, don't! One person is eating, one person is talking, then the person eating has to respond with food in their mouth, and it gets gross and awkward. There are better things to do.

Here are my first-date suggestions, broken down into easy-to-follow categories:

WHERE TO GO: Go for a walk or an easy hike. Pick someplace where you can spend either an hour or three hours, depending on how the date goes. If it's bad, you have an easy exit. The walk ended. If it goes well, you can keep walking or go someplace and get a smoothie. I also like bowling or laser tag, both of which allow you to have fun and get flirty as you compete.

WHAT TO WEAR: Comfortable, casual clothes. If you have to dress up, you didn't listen to me about where to go.

WHO SHOULD PAY: Don't go anyplace where you have to think about this.

SHOULD YOU TEXT? I think it's okay to text the other person before-hand and let him or her know that you're excited and looking forward to having a good time. You can even plan out the date together if you're new to this sort of thing. Do you like to hike? No? How about the mall and a smoothie? By the time you're eighteen or nineteen, though, stop texting long conversations. Plan out the date on your own and leave room for spontaneity. Once you're on the date, put away your phone. Nothing says *I'm bored* or *I'd rather be someplace else—or with someone else* more than taking out your phone and tex-ting friends in the middle of a first date.

SHOULD YOU POST PICTURES? No. What did I tell you about your phone?

HOW LONG SHOULD IT LAST? One to three hours. Three hours is on the long side, but that allows for a two-hour movie and an hour to walk around afterward. Don't make the first date any longer. If it's not going well, you have an exit strategy. If it is going well, you will have the anticipation of getting together the next time.

WHAT SHOULD YOU SAY AT THE END? If your date did not go well, there's no harm in making a joke about it. Better to acknowledge that you tried and failed rather than not trying at all. You can still be friends. Agree to wingman each other. If it did work out, you will know what to say. The truth is always the best. "Well, that was fun. I can't wait until next time."

SHOULD YOU KISS? Kissing is the best, but why not leave that till the next time? It's fun to anticipate. One of the things you can text before the date is this: "Just want you to know that no matter how great this date goes, there's no kissing at the end. We don't have to stress about it. And if we have a terrible time, you won't want to kiss me anyway. LOL. Can't wait to see you."

SHOULD YOU TELL YOUR FRIENDS ABOUT IT? No. Let everyone wonder why you didn't show up at the usual place on Friday night. Enjoy the little bit of mystery that you've created.

TODAY WAS AWESOME.
CAN'T WAIT FOR TOMORROW.

EL-A

Everyone that knew me was aware of what made me happy, how I wanted to spend my time, and where I wanted to spend it. With less than two months before the end of eleventh grade—or he11th, as I referred to it—I made a plan on the table. After school let out, my brother and I would spend the summer in Los Angeles. We'd make videos and hang out with other Viners. Those guys, like Jerry and Max, encouraged us to make the move ASAP. It seemed as if Jerry sent the same text every day: "You gotta get out here." My parents green-lit the plan, and by the middle of May I was telling my friends that we were headed west with an excitement that made some people wonder whether I planned on coming back. I didn't—but that was my secret.

Then, as those plans were being made, I got a chance to visit L.A. earlier than anticipated. A woman named Morgan Escobar emailed me about a tour she was promoting in mid-June. She followed up with a phone call, explaining it was called the E.G.O. Tour, and she'd need me there for a week. All of it sounded top-notch, though none of it mattered once I heard the tour was in Los Angeles. At that point, I was in.

I responded with a single word: "SICK!"

The tour overlapped with the second-to-last week of school. It was the week before finals, but I didn't stress about the exams. My parents did, of course. However, once they saw my B average wasn't moving up or down no matter how I did on the tests, they gave me permission to go on the trip, and within no time I was sailing across the country at thirty-five thousand feet. I was eager to meet up with the other big Viners on the tour, including Brent Rivera, Lance Stewart, Alexander Holtti, Liza Koshy, and Tasia Alexis. It was going to be a helluva week.

As the plane made its final descent toward the airport, my face was glued to the window. The city stretched out forever, seemingly painted on the ground and framed by mountains, desert, and the ocean. Outside, the weather was perfect. I remember looking at my watch; it was 2 p.m. It was a Sunday, and it was sunny that day. I could feel the energy in the atmosphere, and I knew this was going to be a worthwhile adventure.

A car picked me up outside the airline terminal and took me to the hotel. I had none of the bearings I do now, like where Santa Monica is in relation to downtown L.A. or where Hollywood stops and starts. At the time, the city felt big and overwhelming and exciting—that more than anything. I looked for the famous HOLLYWOOD sign. I expected to see it rising from the ground like a giant magnet pulling future Angelina Jolies and Ben Afflecks from across the country. Of course it wasn't like that—but pretty close.

After checking in at the hotel, where I had my own room (snap), I quickly met up with all the other Viners on the tour. We started messing around, making videos. It was super fun. We walked around in a pack, talking and recording Snapchats. The funniest part was when we walked up to the drive-thru intercom at a Burger King without being in a car and tried to order. The guy working there wouldn't help us.

"You need to be in a car," he said.

We pretended to not speak English.

"You can't order here without being in a car."

"We don't have no car."

"That's what I mean. Come inside."

"How we get inside without car?"

"You walk."

"Yes, we walk here to get six Whoppers and six French fries—"

A bus drove us all to Hollywood the next day, where we met up with the promoter, Morgan. I got a sense of her intense focus and what it took to organize such an event and deal with so many personalities as she explained our schedule for the entire week. It was set to culminate on Saturday afternoon with a meet-and-greet with fans at a local mall. Then, at night, we were going to perform in a talent showcase, which sounded an awful lot like a play—at least as Morgan explained it. We were going to have to play characters and memorize lines. And according to Morgan, people from Nickelodeon were going to be in the audience, scouting for talent, which was, she emphasized, a big deal.

But that big deal created a problem. The next day we gathered to practice for the showcase and discovered it was indeed very much like a play. It was a bunch of short skits, with each of us playing different characters. The first time we got onstage to practice, it was apparent that none of us had acted before. It wasn't our fault. We were social-media pranksters and jokesters, not actors. Morgan had never asked if we had performing experience. She had assumed the best and discovered something different.

Fortunately, she was a patient woman and accustomed to solving problems, and that's what she did. After watching us struggle through the rehearsal, messing up our lines and bumping into each other, she got up from her chair, stood in front of the stage, and told us to stop. I sensed everyone's relief.

"Oh sh*t," she said. "You guys suck."

"That's just your opinion," I joked. "Maybe others will be better."

"No, you guys suck."

We all laughed nervously, since we were stuck there. Morgan was already on her cell phone. She booked us an acting coach, starting the next day.

"You guys are going to work at it until you get it right," she said in the same tone of voice my dad used when he was about to ground us. "I'm selling tickets. Nickelodeon is going to be there. By Saturday night, you will not suck anymore."

That sentiment was echoed the next day when our new acting coach spoke to us. When I heard *acting coach*, I expected to be taken to an office building or school-like building, met by someone at the door who'd say, "Welcome to blah-blah-blah acting school," and then ushered into a theater. Instead, we were dropped off in front of a small, Spanish-style house in a normal-looking neighborhood and led through the backyard and into a tiny guesthouse—a single room, actually—that had a bunch of chairs in it. Unsure what to do, we all sat down and waited, talking amongst ourselves until we heard the creaky door handle.

A moment later, our acting coach walked in. She was an older, heavyset woman who reminded me of a gym teacher you don't want to get.

"I heard yesterday was the worst piece of acting ever attempted onstage," she said. "I can't even say there was a bright spot. Not from what I heard from Morgan. But that's okay. We have until Saturday to get this right."

She paused. A tear may have even formed in the corner of her eye. The room got very quiet.

"Morgan's not even paying me to do this. I'm doing this because I love her."

She paused again. The tear disappeared. The drill sergeant returned.

"We're going to have to spend some time. I hope you're ready, because I don't give a f*#k how long it takes—as long as we're ready by Saturday!"

Tasia laughed. She thought everything was funny. Our teacher didn't. Her eyes narrowed.

"You think this is funny? You think this is f*#king funny?"

Then she snapped out of it. Her body softened and so did her voice.

"All right, let's do it."

She stepped toward us and stopped. She looked directly at one of the guys.

"Did you memorize your lines?"

He shook his head.

"Who memorized their f*#king lines like you were supposed to?" she asked.

I raised my hand—and probably because I did, she didn't call on me until later. When it was my turn, she listened and moved on without making any comments. Since she'd critiqued everyone else, I didn't know whether I was good, bad, or worse, and she didn't care to let me know. She spoke to the group about acting objectives. She asked us to imagine what our characters were like in real life ("Give them a story, give them a personality," she said) and what they meant when they said their lines ("Think about why they are saying their lines"). She described other techniques and gave us tips as the afternoon went on. It was like school—a cram session, to be sure—but after four and a half hours, it began to sound familiar.

Then the teacher abruptly ended class. Apparently she was done and ready for us to get out of her house.

"All right, enough! You guys still suck. But tomorrow we'll meet back here and do it some more and see if we can't make you suck less."

For the rest of the week, we went through that same drill. We showed up with our lines memorized and the teacher criticized us. Her gruff, straightforward manner didn't bother me the way it did some of the others. I wanted to act, and had decided I was going to learn as much as possible from this lady. Besides, my dad was tougher and my football and wrestling coaches had been meaner. I handled her, no problem. Nevertheless, the mood within the group was such that Morgan, the promoter, felt it necessary to come in and give us a pep talk.

The next two days, our fourth and fifth in class, were much better. We hit a groove that appeared to please our drill sergeant teacher. At least her demeanor softened, and by Friday afternoon, when she declared the crash course finished, I thought I detected a hint of a smile on her face as we did one final run-through of our skits.

"You've gone from really sh*tty to a place where I think you're going to be sensational tomorrow night. I think you're ready."

"All right!" someone said.

Tasia laughed.

I high-fived whoever was next to me.

We had worked really hard, and we were psyched to put on a show.

The next day, I woke up and it was Saturday—finally show time. Well, not that fast. Like everyone else, I couldn't help but think about the talent showcase that night at the world-famous House of Blues in Hollywood. We had worked hard to prepare, and it was like studying for a big test. We wanted to get to it. But first was the afternoon meet-and-greet with fans at the Westfield Century City mall, and that event quickly overwhelmed all of us.

I had spent the week promoting the tour on Vine, Twitter, and Instagram, as had the others, and though all of us anticipated a good-sized crowd, we didn't know for sure. On the drive there, we guessed how many people might show—five hundred, a thousand, maybe more, maybe less. As we turned the corner next to the mall, we saw about three hundred girls waiting in a line, and that immediately livened up the conversation on our bus.

"Whoa! That's a lot of people," I said.

"We aren't even there yet," someone commented.

"We aren't?" I said. "Wow."

Wow, indeed. That first glimpse of the crowd was the outer edge of the mall. Once in the underground parking lot, we saw another three hundred girls lined up. All of us were amazed. Then we drove around to an opening near the employees' entrance, and there were two thousand more fans. They saw us and started freaking out.

Inside the bus, we were also freaking out. All eight of us did what social-media stars do—we whipped out our phones, recorded the scene, along with our reactions, and then we posted those videos. None of us had drawn such a crowd before. It was a testament to the popularity of social media.

My brother saw the Snapchats I posted and messaged me back, "Are you kidding me? Insane!"

Excited, we hurried out of the bus and were guided into the space that had been set up for the meet-and-greet. Before the doors opened, we were given instructions, and then, once we were thoroughly prepped, and with security in place, the fans were let in. That was the best part—that initial rush, when I could feel the excitement. I love my fans, and as always, I was excited to meet them, take pictures, and talk. It was cool how much they knew about me and wanted to talk about which videos were their favorites. Even though I didn't recognize each person, social media creates a sense of mutual familiarity, and it was that common bond that made the day such a fun time.

But that sense of familiarity also slowed the pace. After an hour and a half, we'd only gotten to about 150 people. There were still more than 2,500 people waiting outside. So they started bringing in fans by the tens—ten one time, twenty another time. We did that for another hour. Then we took a ten-minute break to eat or chill or do whatever. I chose to meet some of the fans still waiting in line, thinking I'd relieve some of the boredom of standing there for hours. But it nearly caused a riot, and a security guard hustled me away.

"If you want some fresh air, go out the back door," he said, pointing in the opposite direction.

I took his suggestion, but I might have gone through the wrong door, because when I walked outside I found myself in the midst of a hundred fans who were at the end of the line—actually, they were waiting to be escorted to the main part of the line. Anyway, suddenly there was no more line, and pandemonium broke out. I tried to take a few pictures and sign autographs, but the crowd quickly got out of control. With no security nearby, my survival instincts kicked in, and I ran away from the crowd through the mall. Only, when I glanced over my shoulder, they were right behind me.

I darted into a clothing store, which created even more chaos when the fans followed me inside. The place filled up, and I twisted and turned and sidestepped my way back out into the mall. For a moment, it was like being back on the football field. I wasn't scared; it was just crazy. At one point, while dashing through the mall, I took a video and sent it to my brother, who wrote back, "What the hell is happening?"

Though my ten-minute break lasted slightly longer than scheduled, I made it back into the event and resumed signing autographs and taking photos. The event lasted another three hours. Afterward, I sat on our bus, rubbing my chin as if deep in thought, and declared, "Well, that was interesting." It was the only thing understated that entire day. By then, we were driving through Hollywood and commenting on the glitz of the fabled Sunset Strip, until we arrived at the House of Blues. It was time to get ready for our performance.

Backstage, we all nervously practiced our lines. I peeked at the crowd through the curtain, and it looked to me to be sold out. Later, I heard someone say about eight hundred people had purchased tickets. Both Morgan and our acting teacher told us not to think about the crowd and pumped us up with encouragement. They didn't have to say much. Even without the week of training, all of us were hams. We videotaped ourselves every day doing funny, silly, outrageous, and stupid things, and posted them for the world to see.

Once the lights dimmed and we got onstage, all eight of us went for it, and whether we were good or not, our commitment to the material made us genuinely likeable. I started out slightly nervous, which was natural, but after reciting my first line, I settled down, and then, after getting my first laugh, I didn't want to stop. Everyone felt the same way. The show ended too quickly, in fact, and I would've done it all over again if someone had asked. I secretly hoped Morgan was going to suggest an encore when she came up to me backstage. Instead, our happy promoter gave me a congratulatory hug.

"I spoke with the people from Nickelodeon, and they said you and Brent were the best actors."

"That's amazing."

"They want to meet with you when you come back to L.A."

I was stunned. I didn't know what to say. They wanted to meet with me. When I came back to L.A.

I guessed I was coming back.

In the most surreal way, it all made sense.

Then it didn't, when, two days later, I was in a classroom, taking my math final. The next day, it was social studies. Unfortunately, I went through the motions on both. I didn't see the point to any of these tests. My English final was worse. Instead of reading the test questions, I filled in the bubbles and waited until the bell rang. I admit this knowing it's a failure of character. I see myself as someone who gives 110 percent effort in everything I do, and I didn't give that effort at the end of the school year. The only person I cheated was myself. This is a lesson I have since learned. For many of us, school has varying levels of importance, but at the end of the day, it teaches us that we have to work hard—and I didn't.

My last final was in robotics, an elective I'd signed up for at the beginning of the year, thinking I might go on to study engineering in college, like my brother. Now I had a different plan, one that couldn't wait; and after handing in that test, I grabbed my backpack and walked out the door. In the hallway, I took out the wireless speaker I kept in my backpack and cranked the volume until the walls and floor vibrated from the pulsing beats of Lil Wayne's "We Be Steady Mobbin'." It was the perfect song for me at that moment, and though the lyrics are extremely graphic and violent, they reflected the way I was feeling right then—angry, defiant, and just *see ya later*.

THE ONLY PERSON WHO CAN STOP YOU
FROM PURSUING YOUR DREAM IS YOU.

HOPPED OFF THE PLANE AT LAX

It's strange to talk about having a sense of what life should feel like when you're still a teenager, but I had a strong feeling about mine. I gunned the engine of my Jeep and peeled out of Westlake's parking lot for the last time. It wasn't just the start of summer; it was the start of the rest of my life, and I felt it down to my bones. People talk about listening to an inner voice, and mine was coming through loud and clear. It was telling me I belonged in L.A.—and I couldn't wait to get there.

The plan was in place. Two weeks earlier, after returning home from college, Logan and my dad flew to L.A. and rented an apartment near the famed Farmers Market and the Grove shopping mall in West Hollywood. "Bro, our place is dope," he told me after returning home. "You're going to love it." He showed me pictures, and I agreed. As I finished finals, he purchased his beloved purple Challenger, and he and his best friend, Mac, set out on a four-day cross-country drive to our new place. I would meet them there after school let out.

His car was loaded with everything we thought we would need to set up a life in the City of Angels: skateboards, computers, video equipment, motorcycle helmets, a basketball, and fourteen pairs of sneakers. The essentials, obviously. At the last minute, my mom had run out of the house holding several pots and pans. She threw them into the backseat.

"You'll need these," she said.

"Why?"

"To eat!" she said.

"But that's why God created Taco Bell!"

The night before I left, I stayed at my mom's house and invited my three best friends to come over and pull an all-nighter with me. We played basketball till 3 a.m., then video games, and told stories until the sun came up. I didn't know when all of us would hang out together again like this. In theory, Logan and I were going to L.A. for the summer, but I knew it was permanent, and so did my parents, and from the way we all said goodbye, I think my friends did, too.

At 7 a.m., my dad showed up to take me to the airport. My mom stood in the driveway and cried as he backed into the road. My friends waved. To this day I remember looking back and seeing all of them standing at the end of the driveway, as if frozen, watching us drive off. Similarly, I remember pulling out my phone as my dad talked to me about the trip, and rereading my brother's texts to me from L.A.: "It's so cool here. The weather's perfect. And so are the ladies." I was already gone.

Once on the plane, I clicked through the entertainment console in the seatback in front of me and planned to watch a couple movies. But no—staying up all night, along with all the emotions of saying goodbye to family and friends, had wiped me out, and as soon as I leaned back in my seat, I fell asleep.

I woke up about ten minutes before the plane landed. Excited, I put my headphones on and played my song—well, it's Drake's song—"We Made It." I think every important life moment should be lived with music, as if you always have a personal sound track going, and "We Made It" was definitely mine at the moment. It was playing in my headset as the plane's wheels connected with the runway and we touched down with barely a bump.

I couldn't have been more pumped. If the aisle hadn't been crammed with people, I would have sprinted off the plane. I was eager to get going, to say the least, and it took every ounce of self-restraint to keep from telling people to hurry. Then, when I was a few feet from disembarking, I stopped suddenly. *I should record this,* I thought.

I pulled out my phone and recorded myself actually stepping off the plane. And as I did, I said, "Hopped off the plane at LAX with a dream that no one can take away from me. It's a dream that I'll never stop pursuing." That was such a meaningful moment for me, and it still is. Then I raced through the airport to find Logan.

He was waiting outside the terminal in his purple Challenger, which was impossible to miss. I threw my bag into the back, and within minutes we were on the freeway, cruising in the fast lane, obviously.

"Are we going to pass the HOLLYWOOD sign?" I asked.

"No, but it's not too far away from our place," he said.

I rolled down the window and felt the warm wind blow against my face. Just as Logan had said, the weather was perfect, and every car, building, and person I saw looked better in the bright Cali sun than they did back home. Even the Walmart where Logan and I bought silverware and drinking glasses seemed better. I'm sure it was due to being on our own, and even going to the store was an adventure. We had no idea how to set up an apartment. Our parents had always taken care of those details. We'd never had to think about something as simple as where the can opener came from. It was always in the same kitchen drawer. Now we were figuring out all that stuff for ourselves, and right or wrong, or just plain clueless, it couldn't have been more fun.

I'll give you an example. We went to the store to purchase a set of plates, and we were immediately confused. We found some labeled dinnerware, but we didn't know if there were different sets for lunch and breakfast, or whether tableware was for every meal. It was confusing, until a salesperson set us straight: Plates were plates. Okay, so with that in mind, we found one set of six for $20.99 and another set of ten for $24.99. We debated one set versus the other, as well as how much money we had been spending on other essentials. Finally, I told Logan that I had an idea.

"What if we just get one plate and share it? You eat with it and then wash it off, and then I'll eat with it and wash it off. That could work, couldn't it?"

"Why do we even need plates?" he asked. "Why can't we eat out of the pot?"

"Because Mom wouldn't—"

I stopped mid-sentence.

"You're right. Why do we even need plates?"

It took about five days to get fully situated in the apartment and ready to live, since we weren't going to shop like this ever again, and when we were done I declared our place "sick." "This is real, Los Angeles," I Snapchatted—and it truly was mind-blowing. Our building was so close to the CBS Television City lot that I could've thrown a baseball all the way to the studio where they taped *The Price Is Right*. We lived above a health food store that was a hangout for actors and models. Everyone was hot. No, that's not really accurate. Some people were super hot. One day I noticed a brunette in workout clothes hurrying down the hall.

"Is that?" I asked my brother.

"That's her." He nodded.

And that's the way we got to know Amanda Cerny, the former *Playboy* Playmate turned Vine star and actress. Logan and my dad had met her when they were looking for apartments, and now she lived two floors below us—and besides being super gorgeous and hot, she was hilarious on camera and off, and really nice. I'd been in L.A. less than a week and found myself living above one of the most popular social-media stars on the planet. I had to remind myself this was really happening.

I also had to remind myself to check in with my mom, and when I finally did she let me know that I'd waited too long to call.

"Are you alive?"

"No."

"What's been keeping you so busy?" she asked.

"We moved in and live above a *Playboy* Playmate."

"You boys are funny."

After Logan and I scoped out the neighborhood, it was time to focus on work. That's why we had moved to L.A. to begin with. I didn't need any more prodding. I was ready to conquer Hollywood. Despite being a seventeen-year-old in sweatpants, I was ready to let the industry know that I had arrived. I didn't know what I was doing from one day to another, other than every day was an opportunity to do what I loved.

Our goal was to collab with a bunch of people. Luckily the only people we knew in L.A. were other Viners and social-media personalities like ourselves, so it wasn't hard to get started. Even though Logan and I were some of the biggest Viners, we hung out with even bigger stars—the biggest, actually, including King Bach, Curtis Lepore, Christian DelGrosso, Brittany Furlan, Rudy Mancuso, Marcus Johns, Nash Grier, and others. As the youngest and lowest on the Vine totem pole in terms of followers, I was always the cameraman. I understood why, and I was like, "Whatever. You can be in my videos and you don't have to put me in yours."

Ideas flew. Laughs were immediate. The long hours we put in

never felt like work. It was like that saying, "If you do something you love, you'll never work a day in your life." After shooting all day, we messed around at night on scooters, go-karts, and motorcycles. This was the dream life, and then, suddenly, it felt like even more of a fantasy. I noticed we had a new follower: singer Ariana Grande. Before we'd gotten used to that, other stars followed, including rapper T-Pain and Justin Bieber.

For two ordinary guys from Cleveland, this was amazing and too much to comprehend, other than it was random and awesome. Justin Bieber? The biggest star in the world? He'd watched our videos—and liked us? Did this mean we were about to blow up? I knew we were part of something new and big—like the early rappers before us—and Hollywood, it appeared, was ready to open its doors to us social-media kids. Logan already had a manager, a lawyer, and a financial advisor, and he was meeting with agents and going on auditions.

And me?

I was having the best summer of my life, but I came to realize that wasn't enough to get me where I wanted to go.

10 THOUGHTS I'M HAVING RIGHT NOW

1. Who wants to go to dinner with me?
2. Black bikinis.
3. Always ready for the gym.
4. Hard work beats anything.
5. Can't worry about what everyone else is doing.
6. I wish my truck had wings and could fly.
7. It always feels good to sleep in your own bed.
8. People really confuse me.
9. Thumbs-up to friends.
10. I can't believe it. I won the Powerball![23]

---

23 Kidding. I'm just practicing for when I do win. What would you do if you won? DM me.

THE EPIPHANY

Midway through our first week in Los Angeles, Logan and I had decided we weren't going back home. We were shooting video in the local park at 3 a.m. when I turned to him and said, "Dude, this is so amazing. We're never going back." He nodded. "I know." We were committed to the big-picture opportunity, and neither of us was going to realize it if we returned to our lives back in Ohio—him to his sophomore year of college and me to twelfth grade. We informed our parents via text and braced for their response.

It turned out they'd anticipated this news, and they responded simply, "Yeah, we know," with one condition. While Logan was of age and could leave college if that's what he chose to do, I was still a minor and had to finish school. My parents made that clear: They didn't want "high school dropout" in the family or on my résumé, and neither did I. Once summer ended, I signed up for online courses and got my diploma six months later. My mom flew out to L.A. to celebrate. There's a video online. Look it up.

By this time, Amanda Cerny had become the big sister we never had. One of our very close new friends in L.A., she collaborated with us on videos and hung out. Every time she stepped into our apartment, she stopped in the entryway and shook her head at the mess, looking as if she wanted to avoid anything that might be contaminated. "I'm so glad I don't live with you guys," she said.

What she was really saying was our apartment was a pit, and I guess it was. Things didn't get put away as much as they got put someplace: clothes, socks, various tennis shoes, video equipment, and whatever props we'd dragged inside, they all were strewn across the floor, set on shelves, and deposited on the furniture. We treated our place like a set, and nothing was off-limits or too crazy when it came to getting the shot we wanted, as was evident by the holes in the walls and scuff marks across the floor.

Amanda never got used to it and always reminded us that we'd have to pay, eventually.

"Why? What's the problem?" we said. "We don't see anything wrong."

She laughed.

"Your security deposit is so massively gone."

One day, as she looked around, she opened the door to our balcony and saw it was crammed with go-karts. We'd gotten a bunch for free from a brand deal we did, and we stored them on our tiny balcony. It was like a horizontal parking lot. We also had surfboards, skateboards, and other stuff wedged into the space. "Boys!" she declared, before asking me if that had been me doing 360s on an electric skateboard on the quiet street next to our building at three in the morning. I nodded yes.

"Oh my God, wear a helmet," she said.

Then it was my turn to tell Amanda to wear a helmet. She cruised into our apartment one afternoon standing on top of what looked like a sideways skateboard. It was electric. Logan and I were like, "Whoa, what the eff is that?" I sprang off the couch, where I was editing a video, and went nose-to-nose with Amanda, my hand out, ready to push her off and jump on myself. But I was actually too polite to do that.

"Can I try it?" I asked.

"No," she said.

"What is it?"

"A hoverboard," she said.

"What?"

"A hoverboard. It's new. I think I'm one of the first people to have one."

"Can I try it?"

"No, you guys break everything."

"Can I try it?"

Amanda realized she was on the losing end of this conversation and stepped off her hoverboard. I put my foot on it, got my balance, and zoomed off down the apartment building hallway, then into the elevator and outside, where I experienced the magical thrill of moving without moving. A few minutes later, I glided back into the apartment, grinning like a kid with a new favorite toy.

"It's amazing," I said. "And it still works!"

Amanda taught us to eat healthier. When we first began hanging out, she was shocked by the way Logan and I ate—or more specifically by *what* we ate. At the time, our diet consisted primarily of chips, pre-workout power drinks, and occasionally fast food, when we needed a "real" meal. But Amanda lived a super-healthy lifestyle, and she took us into the health food grocery store at the bottom of our building and told us to cut out processed foods and go organic, if possible.

Such advice earned Amanda another fan in my family—my mom. When she flew out to L.A. to visit us, she ended up spending nearly all her free time talking to our pretty neighbor. It made sense, I suppose. As Amanda explained, "She's only got guys in her life. She wants to talk about girl stuff."

Every day, we were all about meeting people, collaborating, hanging out, and figuring out L.A. We made Vines all day. It was pretty easy to focus, since Snapchat wasn't big yet and Instagram was more of a support tool than a primary focus. We grew our followers and searched for brand deals. The more followers we had, the more opportunities we'd get, and the more money we could charge. It seemed like a simple formula, and easy for those of us who'd gotten in early.

People were spread out across the city. To collaborate, we went to each other's places, which usually meant meeting new people. The hype around all of us social-media kids was growing, and that drew people that wanted to be in business with us in some way. Investors, producers, directors, actors. At the end of June, I met Saxon Sharbino, a cute blond actress who invited us to a party at her parents' house in the Valley. It wasn't like any party I'd gone to back home. People were dressed up, the food was catered, and the setting around the pool, lit in soft green tones, was straight out of a movie.

The two of us liked each other, and we started talking. She helped me shop for a car. I'd never bought anything as expensive before, but I needed a car to get around L.A. After an exhaustive search of Craigslist, I found a metallic gray Mustang with racing stripes in near-perfect condition. It fit all my criteria: It was fast, loud, and affordable.

Saxon also arranged for me to meet her friend Remi, who quickly became my best guy friend in L.A. He made a living as a singer and a singing coach, but he was one of those multitalented, smart, charismatic people who was good at everything he did. His nickname was Krazy Remi, and it stemmed from his passion for being a thrill-seeking daredevil—skateboarder, snowboarder, and motorcycle stunt rider.

If something had wheels, if it could be taken over a jump, turned around a corner, ridden up a hill or down a mountain, Remi did it to the extreme, and because I loved all that kind of stuff, too, Saxon knew we'd click, and she was right—we did. At night, Remi and I rode motorcycles and skateboards. His riding skills were insane. He taught me how to drift around corners in my Mustang. I was a terror on the empty streets at 3 a.m. I might as well have been in a *Fast and Furious* movie.

Remi also opened my eyes to the business side of Hollywood. Though I applied myself full-time to making videos during the day, I didn't understand how Hollywood really worked. Remi's mother owned a record label, so he had grown up in the business, and he knew all about agents, managers, contracts, and companies, and he shared that knowledge with me, like a tour guide explaining the local customs in a foreign city.

I always had questions for him, and we had long talks about what it took to be part of the entertainment industry. The education he provided opened my eyes to new realities about the business—namely, that it was a business—and as a result, when I took an honest look at myself, I saw a kid who needed to get more serious about his career.

I'd arrived in the city thinking I was bigger than I really was. Us social-media kids were hot and people wanted to meet us, but in reality we weren't as big as we thought. I certainly wasn't. Let me put it this way: If Bradley Cooper was at the top of Hollywood's food chain, I was a bag of chips on the back shelf of a small mom 'n' pop grocery store. My brother was ahead of me. He was the equivalent of an impulse item at the checkout stand, like a candy bar or a pack of breath mints.

I was still doing okay. I was making Vines, getting brand deals, and having fun. For a seventeen-year-old, it was a dream. But I'm a perfectionist, a hard person to satisfy, and I'm hardest on myself.

Once my eyes were opened, I kept looking around and asking myself questions, like what was I really doing? And was I doing enough of the right things? There was a week when Logan's schedule was full of auditions and meetings, and by comparison, I didn't know what I was doing the next day. I didn't have auditions or meetings, or homework or even a curfew. It was a real wake-up.

Though I worked hard on my Vines, I was also waiting around for something to happen to my brother, so maybe the same thing would happen to me, which was the way it had always been with me. I followed in his footsteps. If he played football, I played football—and tried to do it better. If he wrestled, I wrestled—and tried to surpass his achievements. He taught me everything. He is the greatest big brother in the world. But I realized that wasn't going to work in Hollywood. I couldn't ride his coattails. I had to make my own mark.

The other thing that really got to me was the lifestyle. When we all met up at the end of a long day, a lot of people—given their ages, and their freedom—would smoke and drink. Neither of those vices have ever been my thing, and just hanging around people doing that was a time-suck I couldn't afford. I said to myself, *All right, I need to immediately take myself out of this scene. I can't get caught up in it. Instead, I'm going to wake up earlier, work harder, edit more, think of more ideas, and shoot new videos.*

Whatever it was, I needed to do my own thing—and be my own person. I saw my life as it was right then, at that juncture, very clearly. I was on my own now. I needed to branch off from my brother. I had to get real. I needed to grow, get better, learn, and refine whatever natural ability I had. And then, like with football, I had to get in the game.

Once in the game, I had no doubt I would score.

AMANDA CERNY: 5 THINGS I KNOW ABOUT JAKE THAT YOU DON'T

1. He is completely wild and very outgoing, but he's so sweet. He'll do anything for his friends. He likes to take care of people. He's always willing to be there for you.
2. He's business-oriented. Though he comes across as a crazy kid, he actually has a strategy behind everything he does.
3. He's very different than his brother.
4. I love his parents. Jake and Logan's sense of humor comes from their dad, and their mom is so cool and relaxed. Even though his parents are divorced, they're still such a close family. It's very cool.
5. He's a cute boy. He's hilarious. He's in great shape. In the gym, he's a workout animal. But all that's pretty obvious. Something you don't know about him? Well, I called him yesterday to collaborate on a video and he was in San Francisco. Jake, call me back.

WHO'S HUNGRY?

ONE GIGANTIC BALL OF POSSIBILITY

The L.A. summer was a hard season to resist, but I spent most weekdays on the sofa, immersed in work. I was usually sitting amidst a mess of papers, with several different windows open on my computer screen—a video or two that needed editing, new ideas brewing—and my phone, which buzzed constantly. Friends streamed through the door all day asking variations of the same thing—if I wanted to go out and do something—and my answer to them was indicative of where my head was at the time: "Sorry, I gotta work."

Though work had always been my thing, I was trying to take it to a new and more sophisticated level. I wondered if I should be getting paid more for my brand deals, if I negotiated hard enough, or smart enough, and through asking people questions, I learned about pitch decks. So I taught myself PowerPoint and then made a pitch deck about me, one that explained who I was, what I did, my reach and engagement across social-media platforms, and the value of all that information.

It was a way to distinguish myself from others in social media. Instead of being thought of as one of those kids making crazy videos, I wanted to be regarded as a professional, as a businessman. When one of my videos did exceptionally well, I sent it to marketing companies with a note that said, "I can do something like this for your clients.

Your brands could be in videos like these, and getting these results, with this demo." Every day, I tried to go above and beyond the norm.

I also signed up for acting classes. Logan was going to acting workshops to help him prepare for auditions, so naturally I decided to do the same thing. But I didn't know which teacher to choose. Hollywood was full of advertisements for acting classes taught by renowned teachers, and though I'm sure not all of them were legit, they sounded good to me. I thought Logan's teacher was the safest bet, though, but when I mentioned his name to an agent I'd met, she said, "He's excellent, but you should be with Marjorie Ballentine."

"Who's she?" I asked.

"A very well-respected teacher in Hollywood."

"Okay," I said. "But why her?"

"You won't be able to charm her."

I laughed.

"No, seriously. She will kick your ass."

She did, too. The first time I showed up I was extremely nervous. I didn't know what to expect or the types of people who would be in the class with me. As it turned out, I was the youngest person in the class by at least five or six years, with the oldest students seemingly like they were in their forties or fifties. I'd expected everyone to be hot and famous. Some of them were super good-looking; others were ordinary; only a few eked out a living actually working full-time as actors. The others waited tables, worked temp jobs, and joked about how hard it was to pay for class.

I sat quietly through that first class and kept my eye on Marjorie, who I liked. Unlike so many people I'd met in L.A. who tried to be cool or affect a certain style, she seemed real and comfortable in her role as a teacher. The class was small, and she was strict, but unlike the teacher I'd had on my first trip to L.A., Marjorie was direct in a thoughtful, helpful way. She explained what the problem was *and* what you needed to do to correct it. With her, everything came down to choices—and making the right choices.

At the next class, Marjorie discovered my social-media fame. It happened the way it always did—someone in class asked what my Instagram was. "I'll follow you," she said. A moment later, she gasped. "What the . . . You have how many followers? I have seventeen. You have more than two million!"

I think that made Marjorie stricter when it came to me. It also made her sound like my old French teacher. During the first month of working with her, she repeatedly found ways to say, "Jake, you can't do those videos forever. What are you going to do when it falls through?" All the scenes we worked on were dramatic. When my turn came, I was nervous to go in front of the class and act, especially in front of older people. The scenes were intense and for the most part beyond my life experiences. I hadn't fallen in love, broken up, started a family, gone off to war, or found myself in any of the other situations we enacted.

Neither did I really know what it meant to act. To me, it meant pretending to be another person and reciting lines that I'd memorized from a script. I didn't understand what it meant when Marjorie talked about getting inside that character, knowing everything about them so I could make the right choices when saying my lines, so they would sound and look and feel authentic. One of the most uncomfortable days was the first time I had to kiss one of the girls. She was older and more experienced, whereas I was awkward and nervous. But I let her lead, and I gained a little more confidence.

The toughest day for me was when Marjorie wanted me to get emotional. I can't remember the exact details of the scene, but I was supposed to get to the brink of crying, just before the tears, and I couldn't do it. I'm not an emotional person. She pushed me hard. "Come on, Jake. Come on. Put yourself in that place. Get to where you are hurt and near tears." I couldn't get there. It was a defeat. I hated not being able to do something. I wasn't used to that, and it sucked.

But there were better days. In one class, we were doing scenes where the guys were paired up with the girls. The guys had the harder parts. All the older or more experienced guys, most of whom had been taking the class for longer than I had, were falling short. No one hit the mark. I watched each take his turn and I thought the guys were playing the part the same way I would've; they were making the same choices. I listened to Marjorie's suggestions, and at some point, I finally got it.

Just in time, too. She looked at me and said, "All right, Jake. You're up." I walked slowly to the center of class and joined my partner. I took a breath to get into character and to think about what she'd said, and then I nailed it. Marjorie stood up and gave my shoulder a squeeze. "Nice job."

After that, I felt like I'd earned respect from everyone in the class. They saw that I was working hard. I was probably pretty sh*tty when I started, but now, several months later, I was better. I was growing.

Likewise, Marjorie inspired me. In acting class, you talk about yourself and your life as much as you act. Marjorie told stories about being a young actress, having a kid, working two jobs, going to acting school, and so on. It was all this stuff that she did to survive while pursuing a dream. I remember her saying she only slept five hours a night. I got that she worked her ass off. That resonated with me. I saw that acting wasn't a joke. People made it their lives.

Now it was part of mine.

So were improv classes. I took those, too, and they added to my skill set. My daily agenda was filling up with acting class, improv class, keeping up with social media, reaching out for brand deals, and meeting people. Then I began going out on auditions—which, I have to emphasize, is not for anyone with a sensitive ego. Auditions are like buying lottery tickets. You step up to the counter and give someone two bucks, wanting to win, believing the universe might bless you with fortune, but also knowing the odds are you are going to lose.

As for auditions, I had become friendly with Alex Shekarchian, who would eventually become one of my managers. I'd met Shekarchian at an agency party and learned to trust him, and he offered to help get me in the door. He worked independently, rather than for a large firm. Alex believed in me, and told me he would like to introduce me to people in the industry he thought should be aware of me. He began introducing me to casting directors, directors, writers and producers.

My first appointment was a general meeting with Nickelodeon. I met with a few people there and did a scene. I did well, and they, in fact, remembered me from the E.G.O. Tour showcase, but they didn't have any roles for me. The next audition was for a movie called *Nerd*. They had me read the part of a nerdy emotional kid, and I sucked. Plain and simple. I knew it during my performance and had a sour taste in my mouth as I was walking back to the parking lot.

"How'd it go?" Alex asked when I checked in with him.

"I sucked," I said.

"Okay, don't stress. We'll get the next one. What did you learn, though?"

I realized my mind-set was this: Go on a hundred auditions and book one. I didn't need to book every role that I went on, and realistically, I wouldn't. No one does, so I kept any disappointment at home. There was no need to take that with me. No need to think, *Oh, I'm a crappy actor. I'm not good enough to make it big.* Instead, despite the constant beat of thanks but no thanks, I stayed positive. I knew the only thing I could control was me and my attitude. I decided to play the game that way: to keep going out, to keep trying, and to keep getting better.

Next, Alex sent me in to meet with casting directors from a big studio. They later called me in for a huge feature film to play the lead . . . let's just say I would've been playing a superhero. After feeling like I blew this audition, I called Alex and said, "I sucked again."

This time Alex responded with a more stern tone.

"Jake, do you want this? There are a ton of people who want this. *You gotta want it.*"

I didn't even have to think about it for a second. Of course I wanted it. I knew that more than I knew anything. How could this person who believed in me so much doubt whether I wanted this? That's when I realized that it wasn't enough to want something, but I really had to put in the work and show it.

I started focusing on acting like I did my workouts and my Vine videos. I gave it 100 percent. I started taking more acting and improv classes, and I took each audition as an opportunity to learn. Unsurprisingly, with all the work and effort I was putting in, I got better.

In the background, I could hear my old freshman football coach saying, "Adapt and overcome." That wasn't the only echo I heard from high school. Ironically, I'd begun asking myself the same question my French teacher had asked. What was I going to do after the videos? They weren't going to last forever. The reality of being Vine famous was that Vine wasn't going to stay hot forever. In fact, it was already starting to fade compared to Instagram, which was red-hot, and Facebook, which was making a comeback, not that it had ever gone away. Whatever it meant to be famous on social media, whether YouTube or

Facebook or Twitter or Instagram, was still being figured out. It was all too new for anyone to know what was next, other than that something would be next.

I took meetings with Pasquale "Paulo" Rotella, who founded a huge EDM company called Insomniac that produces the Electric Daisy Carnival every year in Las Vegas. And the people at The Collective. And creative people at Studio 71. I picked their brains and tried to absorb everything they said. I realized I wanted to be an entrepreneur behind the scenes as much as I wanted to work in front of the camera. I loved the idea of creating something that was bigger than what I could do on my own. I also loved—

You know what it all was?

As I'm sitting here in the Greenleaf restaurant on Hollywood Boulevard, working on this chapter, I realize what it all was; I realize what was going on with me at the time and what I want to convey to you. The classes, the meetings, the videos I made, the people I met, being in this new city, the auditions—I was experiencing the extreme wonderfulness of life as one gigantic ball of possibilities.

I'd made choices. I wasn't hanging out at night with other social-media kids after spending all day making videos. I was hitting the gym, then getting to sleep so I could wake up early and work. I wasn't following in my brother's footsteps. I'd consciously turned to the left and decided I was going to do my own thing. Once I did that, stuff started to happen.

Yeah.

Life was a gigantic ball of possibilities.

OMG, SO HOT!

WHY DON'T YOU BE LIKE DR. DRE?

With the business thing stuck in my head, I had some conversations with a friend of my dad's, who was a successful businessman back in Cleveland. He'd helped my brother and me navigate some of our deals as they became more complex. I began calling him just to talk about the business side of the business. He explained ideas and terms I picked up from people I met in Hollywood. It was helpful to have someone experienced to share my thoughts with even if they weren't fully formed yet. They were kernels of ideas.

One day, I was on the phone with him, updating him on what I was doing, when I began to ramble. "I want to do something with business. I don't know what it is. I know social media is at the start of something. If I can do something with it now and be ahead of the curve, it could be huge."

He laughed.

"Why don't you be like Dr. Dre? Sign other people like you and make them famous."

I was quiet—an idea was taking shape.

"Yeah! I get it. That actually sounds cool."

"Could that work on social media?" he asked.

"I'm thinking," I said. "I mean, with songs, it's easy. You put someone on your song and it blows up. Dr. Dre did that with Eminem. Then Eminem did it with 50 Cent. And so on. It kept on growing."

"He built a stable of artists."

"That's a sick idea."

"Could you do that with social media?"

"Yeah, but I don't know if it would work."

For the next month, I thought about it every so often—okay, I thought about it like fifty times a day. No matter what I was doing, whether I was working out or in a meeting, the idea popped into my head, which told me it was a good one. Indeed, it played off the basics of building followers on social media, like collabs. Someone with a lot of followers helps someone with fewer by exposing them to a new and larger audience. The problem was, I didn't have the necessary knowledge: I didn't know how to set up a company, how to sign someone to a contract, or if I did manage to get those things done, whether it would actually work to scale once put into practice.

But none of that stopped me.

After much thought, I saw that the only way to learn was to try it, to create a proof of concept test, and legalities aside, it didn't seem especially hard. I needed to find someone—not just anyone but someone who was talented, young, good-looking, funny, already making Vines, and cool to hang out with, since we'd be spending a lot of time together.

I spent a few weeks searching Vine for someone who met my specifications. I found two brothers—twins, actually—from New Jersey. Only fifteen years old, they were good-looking, funny, and cool. I kept watching this one video of them doing crazy physical stuff on a wrestling mat in their garage. It made me laugh, as did many of their videos. In a way, they reminded me of Logan and myself a few years earlier. In my head, I was like, "All right, these kids are super talented. But I don't know how to reach out to them."

A part of me also wondered if I really wanted to talk to them. Do I really want to get involved in this idea? What do I even say? "Come to Los Angeles and make videos with me"? I didn't know how they'd react to that. Or how their parents would react to it. When I said it out loud, it sounded kind of weird. But still, I couldn't get it out of my head.

About a week later, I went home to Cleveland. I hung out with the close friends I'd had over before leaving for L.A. They caught me up on their summer, and I told them about my acting and improv classes and the videos I was making. One night I was hanging out with this girl who was kind of a Viner. She had close to twenty thousand followers. As we talked, she was on Snapchat, and I noticed her Snapchatting with some kid that looked vaguely familiar. I asked who it was and she said, "Oh, it's Grayson Dolan and his twin brother, Ethan."

"What?" I took hold of the hand she was using to cradle her phone and moved it right up next to my face so I could see better. "Oh sh*t! Those are the guys."

"Who are the guys?" she asked, confused.

"Those guys on your Snapchat," I said, explaining why I was freaked out.

"They're twins," she said. "They're from New Jersey. They're so funny and cute."

"Do you know 'em?" I asked.

She nodded.

"I mean, obviously you do," I said. "Let me Snapchat with them."

So I Snapchatted them, and they freaked out.

"Oh my gosh! You're Jake Paul. We love your videos."

I decided to make the pitch then and there.

"Yo, guys, come to Los Angeles whenever you have a four-day break from school. Come out, and we'll make Vines together. I'll introduce you to all the Viners. I'll teach you stuff."

I basically said the same thing that Jérôme Jarre had said to my brother when he invited him to New York. I didn't know what else to say, since I didn't know the plan beyond getting them to L.A. to make Vines with me and see if I could make them famous. They responded immediately. "Dude, we're so down to come." There were details to work out, like they were in school, but I said, "All right, text me when you're ready."

About a month later, Grayson and Ethan called from Arizona, where they were on a tour, and they said their mom could drive them to L.A. when it finished. It worked out perfectly. Several days later, she dropped them off with Logan and me, and for the next four days, Grayson and Ethan and I (and occasionally Logan) made Vines together, tweeted each other, took pictures, and tagged each other on Instagram and Snapchat.

They were super cool, I thought. Total bros. In fact, Grayson and I made a Vine on the evolution of the word *bro*.

"What's up, brother?" I said.

"What's up, bro?" he said.

"What's good, brosky?"

"S'up, brah?"

"Brah!"

"Br!"

Thinking about that video now, it was less an evolution of the word than a six-second de-evolution. Anyway, we all vibed, and I think it came across on camera. Fans responded as I'd hoped. Our "Brosky" Vine had more than two hundred thousand views. A "Dance Battle" video received more than seven hundred thousand likes. "I love when you guys are together," one person wrote. There were thousands of similar comments. The brothers exploded across social media. Their followers on Vine went up tenfold, and they saw similar increases on Instagram, Twitter, and Snapchat. I felt like I'd created a secret formula in my basement. My experiment worked!

The next step would've been to get them to drop out of school as I did, move to L.A., and get to work, cranking out videos and going on meetings. I raised the idea, subtly, but both brothers said the same thing: "My mom's not going to let us unless we make money." Taking that as a challenge, I reached out to Coca-Cola ("Yo, check out these kids. They're blowing up right now") and brought the Dolans their first brand deal for pretty decent money. But it wasn't just about the money for them—their mom insisted her kids stay in school.

I was relieved. I wasn't prepared to sign anyone yet. I didn't have the confidence to be like, "Yo, here's how this is going to work. Here's what you're going to get out of it. Here's where we're going to take it." When I *was* ready, a few months later, toward the end of the fall, the Dolans turned me down. They'd moved on, which I understood. They were blowing up and taking over the world.

It caused a rift in our friendship that was, in retrospect, due to my lack of experience. Those things happen in business. I heard Lil Wayne talk about when Jay Z was trying to sign him to his management company, Roc-A-Fella, and whatever did or didn't go down apparently caused a rift between them. Now, years later, they're all cool, but they might not have been for a short time. That's what happened with me and the Dolan twins.

I continued to work on the blueprint, patterning it after what Lil Wayne did with YMCMB when he signed Drake, who blew up, followed by Nicki Minaj and Tyga. The business model was there. I kept telling the people close to me that I was going to do the same thing on social media. It was a matter of convincing myself more than anything.

After spending Christmas and New Year's at home in Cleveland, I flew to Texas for the Magcon tour. As I had the previous year, I celebrated my birthday with fellow Viners and fans. As it turned out, the Dolan brothers were also among the Viners on the tour. What could've been an uncomfortable situation turned into an opportunity to talk out our differences. Within hours, we were back to being best friends. We cut out the business, enjoyed the excitement of the tour, made Vines together, hung out, and had fun.

As for my eighteenth birthday, people urged me to party hard. But that's not me. Since I don't drink or smoke, the best part of reaching the legal age of adulthood was that I could form my own corporation. I no longer needed my dad to cosign legal or bank documents. So following Magcon, I returned to L.A. and began researching how to create a contract for the people I wanted to sign. I still hadn't met a lawyer who took me seriously and believed in what I wanted to do, so I said, "Screw it, I'll do it myself"—and I did.

I called my company 10 Digit Media. Why? That's the same question my brother, my parents, and my friends asked. The answer? Because there are ten digits in $1 billion, and I was going to build the company with my two hands—in other words, my ten digits. I was obsessed. I talked nonstop about the idea. It was my way of thinking through the challenges of making the idea real. I envisioned a team of collaborators, signing them one person at a time. The bigger the team got, the easier it would be to make someone big. I'd find the first person, then add another and a third, and go all the way till I had a team of ten.

I just had to find that next person.

AIRPLANE MODE

The road to signing my first digital star actually began inside a Cleveland mall two weeks before I moved to L.A. Of course I had no idea at the time that I was going to meet the person who would eventually become the most perfect choice to launch my business. I was still six months away from even beginning to form 10 Digit Media. But Alissa Violet grabbed my attention, as she did that of nearly every other guy who came within sight of her.

It was the day before her high school graduation, and she was shopping for a dress. She noticed a group of about thirty girls gathered near the entrance to the mall, all of them excited and tweeting and posting photos to their Instagrams.

"What's going on?" she asked.

"Jake and Logan Paul from Vine were just here," a girl said. "They just got kicked out. But they were here for a meet-up."

"And it's over?"

"They're going to the gazebo thingy," another girl said. "In front of the fire department."

"That's just down the road," Alissa said.

"Will you take us?" the first girl asked.

She shrugged. "Why not?" And she drove as many girls as could fit into her car down the road to our next meet-up. Though Alissa was only vaguely familiar with Logan and me, she still stuck around with a friend and asked for a picture with us. I'd already spotted her in the crowd and made sure to angle toward her as Logan and I left the building. When she asked for a photo, I grabbed her phone and put my number in it. Later that night, we began texting and fast-tracked our friendship, since I'd have to tell her goodbye the next week when I moved to L.A.

When I returned for the holidays, I hit Alissa up to hang out. She was my type: way hot and really weird in a funny, relatable way. I'll say this as an aside: I think a sense of humor is a quality that makes anyone hot. If you're funny, you can get any guy or girl you want. But I wanted to talk to Alissa, that's all. I wanted to pitch her on signing with me. She already had several thousand followers on Vine and Instagram, and I watched her Snapchats, where she had a knack for goofiness.

She met me at my mom's house, and we drove to Taco Bell. Uncertain how to bring up the subject directly, I asked what she wanted to do with her life. She said she was in community college to appease her parents, but she wanted to model. I literally clapped my hands together from excitement. That was my opening. I saw her potential as a model; she was tall and blond, with long legs and an athletic, all-American look. I didn't tell her yet, but I saw even more potential for her on social media.

"You have to model," I said. "If that's your dream, you have to do it."

"It's not that easy," she said.

"But if you stay here, you just go along a path that maybe isn't really what you should be doing."

"I know." She sighed, frustrated. "But I'm in school."

"You don't even go. You skip classes."

She laughed, and I kept talking about life in L.A. I told her what Logan and I were up to, about people I'd met, about what it was like to get brand deals and go on tour. As I pulled back into my mom's driveway, I put it all on the table. It was like when I played football and saw a little daylight through the line. I went for it. I sensed she wanted in on the fun and definitely wanted to model.

"Alissa, I'm dead-ass. You need to just come to Los Angeles," I said. "Logan and I will blow you up on social media. You'll start making money from brand deals. I'll get you signed to a modeling agency. Your career will happen. It'll blow up."

"It's not that easy," she said again.

I turned and stared.

"You're wrong. It is that easy."

And it was—mostly. She sent me pictures of herself that I forwarded to someone I knew at Next Management. They wanted to meet her immediately. About a month later, Alissa flew out and stayed with Logan and me for two weeks. She met Amanda Cerny, whom she loved, and we showed her around town. On the day of her meeting at Next, Alissa was extremely nervous. Logan and I walked her in, and within fifteen minutes, she was being offered a contract.

The glitch occurred when she went back home to speak with her parents and their family attorney. One afternoon, as she waited for the thumbs-up, she tried to make a funny Vine. She jumped off a friend's loftlike second-floor balcony and onto a couch one floor below. Unfortunately, she missed the couch and broke her back. The good news was that she was okay, but it delayed her move to L.A. an indeterminate time while she recovered.

I didn't like having to wait, but it didn't slow me down. In addition to my acting and improv classes, I watched TED Talks and entrepreneurial videos. I devoured information of all kinds. I know this might sound geeky, but while friends of mine chased women, I looked for lawyers, producers, and businessmen who'd talk to me. I wish high school had fascinated me as much as business. I couldn't get enough information about it.

My brother was a great partner and inspiration. We talked about writing a movie together that would feature a cast of social-media stars and debut on YouTube instead of in a movie theater. Nothing about it would be traditional other than it would have a beginning, a middle, and an end, and, of course, it would be sick funny. We wanted to be able to do it ourselves and distribute on platforms that reached people like us. In early 2015, this was a novel idea; no one was thinking social media first, movie chains second.

With typical enthusiasm, we pitched it to two guys we'd met, Dylan Trussell and David Dinetz, who owned the production company Culprit Creative. They made commercials for companies like Starbucks and Beats By Dre, and they were super creative and obnoxiously funny, like nonstop, pee-your-pants funny, which was perfect for what we had in mind—a movie called *Airplane Mode*. It would be about a whacked-out bunch of social-media influencers whose plane is headed for a social-media convention and goes down because none of them can turn their cell phones to airplane mode. We were inspired by the original *Airplane!* movie. If you haven't seen it, go online now and watch. The 1980 comedy was packed with classic lines:

Dr. Rumack: Can you fly this plane, and land it?
Ted Striker: Surely you can't be serious.
Dr. Rumack: I am serious . . . and don't call me Shirley.

Our goal was to make a contemporary version of *Airplane!* We thought we could create a hit if we wrote it with the fast-paced comedy in mind. As an afterthought, we might even end up discovering and explaining to the world why you have to put your phone in airplane mode when you fly. Does anyone know why? Does anyone do it?

Working on the script was like a party. The four of us—Logan, Dylan, David, and I—got together twice a week at night, writing from 9 p.m. until two or three in the morning. Eddie and David knew the proper format for a screenplay, all those elements about structure like plot, turning points, and theme, the things you don't think about when watching a movie. As for Logan and me, we supplied the funny and the completely whacked.

After the first line was written, I remember a certain spirit and determination overtook all of us. We just went for it. Any idea was considered, any joke, any gag. Nothing was off-limits or out of bounds. We had one goal: Make it so funny that half the audience would slide out of their chairs laughing, and the other half would have to hit pause on their computer and run to the bathroom. Slowly but steadily, the pages piled up. Every twenty pages or so, we went back over them and tried to inject even more funny.

In the meantime, life got crazy—really crazy. I'm talking so much activity and things popping that I can barely remember the order in which it all happened. Other than working out at night and waking up early to answer emails, everything else was a blur. But let me try to make some sense of it, if only to get it straight in my own head. Seriously, I haven't paused to think about how I got from there to here until right now. So:

That spring, as we finished *Airplane Mode*, my brother's manager began to canvass the industry for deep-pocketed investors with an immature sense of humor. I auditioned for, and got the part in, a digital movie called *Mono*. It was a teen comedy about a school where the nerds rise to the top of the food chain after all the cool kids come down with mono. I was only on set for eight days, but it was real experience in front of the camera with a director, who provided instruction between takes, and it helped me grow a ton as an actor.

Then Logan and I moved into a two-bedroom apartment in a modern-style building on Hollywood and Vine (I'm not kidding), which quickly became home base for a key group of social-media influencers. We followed our friend King Bach there. He'd had an apartment in the building since before Vine came out, I think, and he put out the invitation to other influencers to move in. It was a great location, right in the center of Hollywood, amid all the nightlife, restaurants, and hangouts. The W Hotel was next door. There was a Trader Joe's on the corner. The building had a top-notch gym, a sweet pool, a rec room with pool tables, and tons of places to hang out. The week Logan and I decided to move in, Amanda Cerny advised us to just run away from our old apartment before the landlord or the health department saw the way we had destroyed the walls and floor shooting videos there. She was only half joking.[24]

We decorated our new place with a bunch of beanbag chairs, a massive flat-screen TV, beds, and desks. It was more like a studio where we worked and slept than anything resembling an apartment.

---

24 Amanda says, "I wasn't half joking. I wasn't joking at all. There's no way they were getting any of their security deposit back."

My mom flew out to check on our new setup. She left satisfied that we were safe, but stressed by what she called a "revolving door of strangers and stunt people."[25] Note to Mom: They were neither strangers nor stunt people. They were friends.

Soon after we moved into our new building, other influencers followed. Our neighbors were a who's who of famous influencers, including Amanda, Curtis Lepore, Rudy Mancuso, Cameron Dallas, Lance Stewart, and others. In this one building were about twenty people with more than a hundred million followers collectively. It was exciting. It was a hotbed of creativity, where I could walk anywhere in the building, inside or out, at any time of day or night, and find someone ready and willing to collab. It was amazing!

Beyond a social-media mecca, I saw a business opportunity. I suggested all of us collab on a line of T-shirts and promote it collectively to our followers. It was a no-brainer, right? Together, we had millions of followers, and we could promote a cool product to them. Companies paid us big bucks to do this. We could do it for ourselves. But no, egos, lack of vision, and lack of ambition outside of anything people thought of themselves thwarted the idea, and sadly it went nowhere.

Looking back, I think part of the problem was that I was the youngest among the influencers. I was Logan's baby brother, and I was still a teenager. Everyone else was in their early to mid-twenties. I didn't have enough juice to persuade the older guys to try something

25 My mom explains: "Their apartment was—and still is—like a frat house. I don't even know how many people live there. Logan and Jake text people when they need someone for a video and ten minutes later people start flying in on hoverboards. One minute I'm taking a bite out of dinner and then the next minute there's a girl lying on the kitchen counter, pretending to give birth to the Easter bunny. Or someone is smashing plates or jumping out of a box."

different. At least I tried, though. I knew the idea was good. It only fueled my determination to get my own team going.

I put in a call to Alissa Violet. In contact daily, I knew her broken back had healed and she was itching to get to L.A. She was ready to get to work. One question remained, and I asked it.

"When are you coming?"

A BRIEF CONVERSATION WITH MY MOM

'm thinking about what my mom said in the previous chapter about the stress our messy apartment caused her, and I can't let it go without getting her back on the phone.

Me: Mom, it's me again.

My mom: Logan? I forgot to tell you that I love you more than your brother today.

Me: Mom, stop! [*She laughs.*] I'm a little offended by your comments about Logan's and my old apartment.

My mom: You guys were slobs. I don't understand why you got rid of the person that came in to clean.

Me: We never had one.

My mom: That explains things. Did you get my Snapchat the other day?

Me: Which one?

My mom: The one that said, "Jake, get rid of that pimple on your face. You need to go to the dermatologist."

Me: Mom!

My mom: Jake, I'm still your mom. Even though I'm back in Ohio, I have to tell you what's important.

Me: A pimple is not important.

My mom: No, but getting rid of it is. Do you know what else is important?

Me: What?

My mom: Paying your traffic tickets. Do you remember how I spent most of the time when I visited you and Logan last month?

Me: Having fun?

My mom: I was at the courthouse, paying your speeding tickets. Your license was about to get suspended because you didn't pay your tickets. When I wasn't standing in line there, I ran around buying groceries and cleaning supplies, and cleaning your apartment—because it's disgusting!

Me: Mom! It's the way we like it.

My mom: Jake, are you getting enough rest? I don't want you burning out.

Me: I'm good. I feel great.

My mom: How about that pimple?

Me: It's good. I just popped it. It splattered all over my phone. Want to FaceTime and see it?

My mom: I'm proud of you.

Me: One quick question. Who do you love more, me or Logan?

My mom: I think you're both great. I think you're both fantastic and amazing. I can't even say who's better.

Me: But if you were to say it?

My mom: Bye, Jake. [*She laughs.*] I have a life of my own! [*More laughter.*]

IT'S AMAZING WHAT CAN HAPPEN
IF YOU ACTUALLY TRY.
AND WHY WOULDN'T YOU?

TEAM 10

It's probably not cool to admit, but when I heard I was among the cast of the movie *Dance Camp* pictured on a giant billboard on Sunset Boulevard, I drove by it not once, not twice, not six times, but several dozen times before I got my fill of *Oh my God, that's me!* I have no idea what cool really means, how you define it, or why people even care, but holy crap, seeing myself up there was cool. It was almost as cool as the experience I had the year before, auditioning for the part.

It was the end of spring 2015, a few weeks before Alissa was scheduled to arrive in L.A., and I got an email from the movie's casting director, John McAlary. He introduced himself and explained that they wanted me for the movie. It was a YouTube Red original about a teen who goes to a dance camp expecting to have the worst summer of his life. Then he meets a girl and beats the dance camp king, Lance (the part they wanted me to play), for the camp's championship. They knew who I was from social media, he said, and they wanted me to come in and test for the part.

A day later, he sent the script, and once I read it, I knew I could play the part. Lance was a cocky, outgoing a-hole, who you were supposed to laugh at more than you were supposed to hate. I knew I could make the bad guy likeable. I spent a week studying the lines and thinking about my approach. It was a good, meaty scene; Lance was squaring off against some dude, ready to fight him. In the actual audition, I played the confrontation as a slow boil, until I just exploded with rage and whipped off my shirt, ready to tangle. But I did it in a way that was funny, and when my shirt came off, the room erupted in laughter.

I couldn't have felt better about everything. Then, at the end, the director, said, "Okay, did you prepare your dance?" I froze and I went from my happy place to panic.

"What are you talking about?" I asked.

"Oh, you didn't know you had to dance?"

"No one told me."

"Lance is the best dancer in the camp. You were supposed to have prepared a minute-long routine."

"Oh sh*t." I shook my head. "Pardon my language."

"We'll just play a song, and you can dance, and we'll see what you got."

Talk about being put on the spot. But I didn't have time to think. The music started. It blasted from large speakers on both sides of the room. I don't remember the specific song, only that it was a pop song I'd heard before, and it had a strong beat, and they were playing it loud. Though I'm not a trained dancer, I had one thing going for me—I don't get embarrassed. So I listened for a moment, felt the beat, and went for it.

If I looked dumb, I didn't care. They loved it!

Three days later I called home to tell my family that I'd gotten the part, my first movie role, and it was because I had danced my ass off. My mom said, "I'm not surprised. Even as a little kid, you had the moves."

Production on *Dance Camp* began in June and lasted more than a month. We shot at an actual campsite in Griffith Park. It was one of the hottest summers anyone could remember. The low-budget outdoor set didn't include air-conditioning, but I enjoyed every day of work, even those when the sweltering conditions made wearing

MY FAVORITE MOVIES

Talladega Nights: The comedy is outlandish, I laughed nonstop, and of course the cars are cool. There are no limits or boundaries in this movie.

Step Brothers: This comedy reminds me of Logan and me, and Will Ferrell's performance combined with the quirkiness of not doing traditional jokes is awesome.

The Dark Knight: Visually, this is a great movie. It's a thriller. And it's got a classic action hero, which is the kind of role I want to play someday. Plus, Heath Ledger as the Joker is crazy.

The Dark Knight Rises: It's all about Bane. His lines and the way he's so evil but so calm about it is why I can watch this movie over and over.

Forrest Gump: There is so much going on within the simplicity of this guy just talking about his life.

The entire *Fast and Furious* series: This is a whole category by it-self, but I have to include it. The first *F&F* movie was the first movie I ever saw; my grandpa took me. He knew about cars. I loved cars. And I've loved every *F&F* movie since. Paul Walker—unforgettable.

my costume—a gold, sparkly tracksuit—a hot, itchy challenge. I took pride in my positive attitude and work ethic. I became instant friends with this guy named Flipz (full name Ivan "Flipz" Velez). He was one of the background dancers, but in real life, he is one of the most respected dancers in Hollywood. If you want your mind blown by how someone can move their body, look him up on YouTube. He was in *Step Up 3D* and *Stomp the Yard.* Just a brilliant guy, full of great energy, and I hung out with him—and still do to this day.

In June, around the middle of production, Alissa finally came in from Ohio. She called as soon as her plane touched down at LAX, and I told her to come straight to the set. Once she arrived and took in the cameras, crew, and costumes, she had the same realization that I'd had a year earlier: Ohio was a great place to grow up, but the future was here in Hollywood. She met my friends, messed around on the set, and danced with us.

Once the movie wrapped, I focused my attention on Alissa. She'd already started to work on her social-media presence while I finished the movie, and with me tagging her in my posts and videos, her followers grew. She learned quickly and stuck to my No. 1 rule: Make awesome content. One of the funniest videos we did was a spoof on MTV's *Cribs*. As Alissa showed the family room, Logan dragged a dead body out. When she opened the fridge, I was on a shelf inside. In another video, she asked if I thought she looked fat in her dress. When I hesitated, she beat me up.

Everyone wanted to collab with her. Getting tagged by the biggest influencers was like cooking with rocket fuel. When she hit 400,000 followers, I got her brand deals with Coca-Cola and Bongo jeans. She was an easy pitch to companies. She made money. Everyone was happy, her parents were relieved, and I got immense satisfaction seeing my second experiment work.

But, as I told myself, it was no longer an experiment. It was a business, and Alissa's success made me eager to keep building my team.

At the end of summer, I began looking for more talent. Within the first ten minutes of searching on Vine, I found Lucas and Marcus Dobre, twins who were incredible break-dancers. Someone I followed also followed them, so their video—it happened to be their first one—showed up in my newsfeed. I watched it several times, each time feeling more certain Marcus and Lucas were perfect. They had

the boyish good looks that fangirls would eat up, and they were funny
and they were talented. I liked the way they incorporated comedy in
their dancing.

I saw potential, and I wanted to sign them. They already had five
hundred thousand followers on Vine, but they needed help on all
the other platforms. I immediately followed both of them on Twitter. After they followed me back, I DMed them, sharing my idea of
Team 10, explaining what I was doing with Alissa and what I'd done
with the Dolan twins, and then of course pitching them on joining
the team.

Though they were immediately down for it, they were young, as
I'd been when I started. They lived at home in Maryland. I spoke with
their parents, who asked questions but ultimately liked the strategy
and let their boys sign with me. By the fall, they started making regu-
lar trips to L.A. We made videos and worked on their other platforms.
I helped them make their Facebook profiles, which they didn't have
yet, and within two months, they went from zero likes to more than
seven hundred thousand.

They were good and blew up on their own. As they soared up
the ranks of premier Viners, they worked extremely hard, something
Alissa did also. They understood that while we all had fun, success
depended on making a serious commitment to extract the best possible effort from ourselves. As I repeatedly said, "We can't just put out
videos and post photos. Whatever we do has to be awesome."

Alissa and Marcus and Lucas got it. They were all in. They worked
as hard as me. It was fun creating a team, being part of one, and seeing my vision take shape.

For the next person I brought onboard, I had a specific type of
person in mind. I wanted the male version of Alissa, a great-looking
guy with a personality that would bridge the inaccessibility of his

looks. One day I was randomly looking through Instagram and saw this guy in a photo with my friend Tanner Zagarino. The guy's name was Neels Visser. I looked at his Instagram page and thought, *He's perfect for Team 10*. Strangely, though, I didn't reach out to him like I did the others. I didn't follow or DM him immediately. I don't know why.

The next day, I was hanging out with Cameron Dallas, and he asked if I wanted to go to a Calvin Klein party that night. I said, "Sure, let's go." Not ten minutes after getting to the party, I spotted Neels there. Cameron knew who Neels was talking to and so we all started hanging out. After a bit, we all agreed the party was too whack, and we went on a run to Taco Bell,[26] where I found out more about Neels—he was a model from Arizona whose family now lived in Newport Beach. I decided he was cool.

A few days later, I invited him to hang out with us. I wanted to see if he'd vibe with Alissa, Marcus, and Lucas. Once I was sure there was chemistry, I pitched him on Team 10. He understood, and right away he was ready to sign on. I spoke to his parents in Newport Beach; they were also supportive. From then on, Neels began driving up to L.A. every day and hanging out with us. Neels was up so frequently, and Alissa was always at our place making videos, taking pictures, and planning next steps with me, that it made sense for both of them to move into our apartment. Lucas and Marcus were in constant touch. We worked to all hours, laughed nonstop, and the creative energy was sick.

We saw results. Marcus and Lucas were huge and getting bigger. Neels blew up. Alissa continued to grow. This idea of mine was working in the way I'd envisioned and then some. It turned into something more than just amassing followers. It was personal. Our fans weren't

---

26 I'm noticing that Taco Bell is a recurring theme in my meetings.

merely entertained by our friendships; they were involved in the relationships. When we went to the beach or sailing, they wanted to know all the details. They asked if anything was going on between Alissa and me, and they wanted to know if Neels and Alissa were dating. They wanted to hang out with us.

Though the living situation was crowded at best—what with Logan and his friend (and videographer/editor) Mark in one room and me, Neels, Alissa, and occasionally Marcus and Lucas in another—we had fun together. The only sacrifice was our privacy, but we shared pretty much every detail of our lives on social media, so other than the fact that Alissa hid her toothbrush and razor, no one minded.

DON'T COMPLAIN.

JUST GET IT DONE.

ALISSA VIOLET: 5 THINGS I KNOW ABOUT JAKE THAT YOU DON'T

1. He always brushes his teeth.
2. He eats pretty healthy but can go on binges where he powers down on donuts and pizza.
3. His workouts are insane. He runs a mile, literally runs it, and then does a hard-core workout with weights and resistance exercises.
4. Jake is a perfectionist.
5. And sometimes he snores.

BIZAARDVARK

Okay, Jake, come on over."

It was November 2015, and a friend of mine was having some people over to his place. He and his roommate lived next door and invited Logan and me to hang out. Later that night, we walked over and joined the party in progress.

It was a mellow scene, a typical gathering in someone's apartment with some food and music—except for one unmistakable detail that made this party unlike any other that night anywhere else. The fifteen or so people hanging out in this ordinary two-bedroom apartment included the most famous twenty-one-year-old in the world, Justin Bieber.

One thing about someone that famous: It doesn't matter whether it's a room of fifteen people or fifteen thousand people, that person is going to be the center of attention, and so it was with Justin. He was definitely the center of this party, and I could tell that he was comfortable with that. It fit his personality. At the same time, he was super chill and super friendly.

Before we were even introduced, he saw Logan and me come in and was like, "Hey, what's up? What's up? I love you guys. Your videos are great." To me, hearing the biggest star in the world say he was a fan was not only a thrill, it confirmed that moving from Ohio had been the right decision.

Then, in case I was looking for more validation of that decision, which I wasn't, I was invited to Kendall Jenner's birthday. The party was at the hottest club in the city, The Nice Guy, and when I arrived, it looked like a small family gathering. All I saw was an intimate group of people, basically Kendall and her mom, her sister Kylie, and maybe a few other friends.

Kendall was breathtakingly beautiful, and tall and sleek, and wearing an outrageously sexy black top and pants. I had to force myself to not stare. But after a few minutes, I said, "Screw it," and gave in to what Mother Nature insisted upon. It was another one of those moments when I was reminded I was no longer in Ohio.

Then, not even twenty minutes later, Kim Kardashian showed up along with her husband, Kanye West. Then Drake entered the party, followed by Gigi Hadid and Tyga. It got better and more unbelievable by the minute. The birthday cake was in the shape of a bottle of Chanel No. 5 perfume, and after I gawked at it, I turned around and found myself face-to-face with DJ Martin Garrix, who looked as surprised to see me as I was him—except he was the one who said, "Jake?"

"Yes."

"Sh*t, man, I love your videos."

By eleven thirty, the relatively small area in the club hosting the party was packed. It seemed everyone on the guest list had arrived. If a bomb had gone off, TMZ and most of the paparazzi in the city would've gone out of business. It also seemed as if everyone was just getting ready to start his or her night—and so I left. That's right—I left.

I found the few people I knew there, bid them a good night, and went home. It was a weekday, and while it's one thing to stay out late on a weekend, the next day was a workday for me. Maybe not for the others at the party; they'd made it. They had their careers, they were thriving, and part of their job as stars was to be out late. But I was just starting to climb the ladder; I barely had one foot on the first rung. I had to stay focused—and I did.

As I headed for the door, someone asked why I was leaving so early. I said, "Oh, I have stuff to do."

More than I knew. In early December, Shekarchian called with news of an audition that he said was perfect for me. I heard the excitement in his voice. Rather, I heard the seriousness of his tone. He didn't ask what I'd been up to, as he normally did. He didn't waste time on small talk. I don't think he even said hello. It was simply: "Yo, Disney wants to meet you and you *need* to go."

"What?" I said. "I need to go?"

"You need to go," he said. "They're requesting you."

"What?"

"Yeah. I think it could be huge for you."

The script arrived the next day. It was for a new Disney Channel comedy called *Bizaardvark*, a show about two teenage girls who are up-and-coming social-media stars who write and play music for their own channel, Bizaardvark. I was auditioning for the role of a more experienced influencer, someone who could mentor the girls through the tricky world of video blogging. I worked on it with my brother's best friend, George Janko, a popular Viner, actor, and musician. He had good instincts and is a natural coach. We practiced it a bunch of times, but the thing was, I only needed to read it through three times before I felt like I had it down.

I remember telling George the part felt familiar. I told him that Dirk reminded me of a nicer version of Lance, the guy I played in *Dance Camp*. Then, after another read-through, I realized the real reason the part came to me so naturally. Dirk was like me. Or I was like him. He was funny, did crazy things, and liked to be everybody's big brother. It was like slipping into a pair of favorite sneakers. The fit was perfect.

"Let's just do it one more time," George said.

I did, and the next day I went to the audition. It was in a strange part of the city, a warehouse district so far from my normal circle of travel that at one point my GPS paused to say, "Jake, are you sure we're going in the right direction?" Even though it didn't seem like it, we were. Although I had already gone in for a general meeting with Disney, this time was like nothing I was expecting. I expected to walk into a typical audition setting, where other actors are waiting their turn and there's a room full of people judging your tryout. It's super intimidating. To my surprise, though, I walked inside and it was just the casting director and me. Apparently this meeting was set up solely for her to meet me and see if I could even read in front of the Disney executives.

"Hi, Jake Paul," she said, walking down a short flight of stairs. "I'm so happy to meet you."

She spoke as if we already knew each other. It turned out she did know my brother's manager, but she also knew everything about me. She'd done her research. "I love you," she said. "And your videos are awesome." Her enthusiasm weirded me out, but then I shrugged and thought, *All right, this girl really likes me—which is cool and a lot better than a rejection.* She wanted to hear me read. I followed her upstairs to a small room.

"All right," she said. "Let's do it."

I took a couple steps backward, to give myself space in the center of the room, and recited my lines. She smiled.

"You're good to go," she said. "I'm going to schedule your meeting with Disney for later this week."

From then on, everything happened fast. The script was messengered to me the next day, and the day after that, I went to Disney for my audition. It was in one of those high-rise buildings whose exterior is all dark mirrored glass. I stepped out of the elevator on the twenty-first floor into a room filled with people auditioning for the series. They weren't necessarily all for Dirk, but I noticed two guys waiting who were obviously there to read for the same part as me. It was the type of scene I'd expected when I met the casting director a couple days earlier. The room was thick with tension and nerves. Everyone eyed each other warily.

After about fifteen minutes, they called a group of us to go through a set of doors, where we waited in another lobby. I looked around and saw I was with the two other guys auditioning for Dirk and two girls that were going up for another role. All of us were competing with each other. The discomfort of being in that room was interrupted when the girls who were already cast as the two main characters, Madison Hu and Olivia Rodrigo, walked into the room and began talking to us. Suddenly, Madison stopped talking to me and cocked her head.

"Hey, I think I know who you are," she said.

"Really?"

"Yeah, I follow your friend Neels. He's really popular on Instagram."

"Yeah, he's blowing up," I said.

Then she typed my name into her search bar. I watched her expression change as she read the results. She showed her phone to Olivia. Both of them slowly turned toward me and stared, slightly freaked out.

"You have more than five million followers on Facebook," Madison said. "And you're at like two million on Instagram."

Despite their reaction, I maintained my focus while the two other guys were called in to read, one at a time. I wanted to stay in the moment and within myself, no outside, unnecessary distractions whatsoever, the way I used to be before a wrestling match. Finally, my name was called. I was ready. I walked into the audition room and found another familiar scene: several long tables pushed together with men and women seated in chairs on the other side, looking me up and down. They studied every movement I made and every inch of the way I looked, from the top of my messy blond hair to the tips of my LeBrons. They were the producers, writers, and network executives.

I played it casual as I approached them.

"Hey, what's up?" I said.

They laughed.

Then I just went for it. I played the part exactly the way I did at my house, and I thought I nailed it. When I finished, they stood up and clapped, the first and only standing ovation I've received that didn't follow a horrendous wipeout on my motorcycle or skateboard. I busted out a megawatt grin; though I didn't want to show too much emotion in the room, I couldn't help it. Not even rapid-fire questions from one of the Disney executives could extinguish my good cheer.

"Tell me about your fans on social media," he said.

"What's the dumbest thing you've ever done?" he asked next.

I paused. Before anything could be read into my silence, least of all a hesitancy to answer, I explained that I had like a million choices to consider. That also got a laugh, even though I wasn't trying to be funny.

Then one final question: "What makes you believe you're the right fit for the Disney family?"

I nodded a moment, then broke out the grin.

"I'm a good kid," I said. "I don't smoke or drink. I work hard. I mean, I really work my butt off. I don't know any other way. And I think I bring value as an actor, as someone who's funny, and as someone who arrives with their own fan base."

Everything I said was real and genuine, and it seemed to register. I saw a few people nod and make notes.

After finishing up the questions, I walked out of the room. As I did, the writers stood up and high-fived me. I took that as a good sign. Outside in the lobby, someone came out after me and without looking directly at the two other guys who'd auditioned before me said, "Everyone can go home except Jake." I tried to keep my excitement in check. As much as I was celebrating inside, I knew the process wasn't over. I knew that, as with anything good, I had to earn it.

Indeed, as soon as the other guys left, they took me back to read with the two girls, Madison and Olivia. They wanted to see our chemistry together. After one read-through, everyone knew we clicked. I read the same scene as before, only this time with Madison and Olivia. Halfway through, they both broke character and laughed so hard they couldn't continue.

"Okay, we'll be in touch," the casting director said after everyone had stopped laughing, dried their eyes, and finished the scene.

Outside, I hopped into my car and cranked the radio. It sounded like Soulja Boy and Drake were in the car with me. I turned 'em up even louder. "We made it!" I shouted with them. It was nighttime now, and I drove around L.A. for a while, wanting to savor the good news, the feeling of triumph, and the really good vibe. My dad was also in town. He'd flown out a few days earlier to visit Logan and me, to check in on us. He was on his way to our apartment when I finally walked in. Logan and his friend George were in the kitchen.

"How'd it go?" Logan asked.

"I got the role," I said.

"You got it?" George said.

"No, not officially. But I killed it. I murdered it."

When my dad arrived, I played a trick on him. Though he didn't know anything about acting, he always advised me to hold my script in my hand during auditions in case I forgot my lines. So when he asked how the audition had gone, I looked down at the floor and shook my head, as if disappointed.

"I forgot my lines," I said. "I thought I had them memorized but—"

"Did you have your script?" he interrupted.

"No."

"I knew it," he said, upset. "I told you to have your script in your hand, in case of something just like that. But you never listen to me."

At that point, I cracked up.

"I'm kidding," I said. "I killed it. I did really well."

I went to one more screen test with the entire cast. I knew this one was the last one. It was do or die. Before I left home, Logan said, "Either come back Dirk or come back on your shield," a reference to *300*, one of our favorite movies. I came back that night as Dirk. I got the part. It was an incredible feeling, knowing that my life might change, yet there was still a chance it might not turn out that way.

"Whatever happens, happens," I said, reluctantly but aware that was the right way to play it.

After four days of biting my nails, Alex called. I was in the gym.

"Are you ready?" he asked.

"What do you mean?" I said.

"You got the role. You're doing it."

"I got it?"

"Do you want it?"

"I totally want it."

"Well, you got it."

•   •   •

Fast-forward two months. I had no idea what I was getting into when I signed up to be on a weekly Disney Channel TV series. What I soon learned after starting work in January was that it was better than I imagined. Granted, on my first day, I wasn't allowed past the front gate; it turned out I didn't have the right pass. Once that was straightened out, I was surprised to find a parking space right in front of the soundstage. Then I saw why the space was empty. There was a sign in front of it that said JAKE PAUL—BIZAARDVARK.

Even cooler: Upstairs, someone was waiting for me. They showed me into a room, my dressing room. It was massive.

"How long are we here for?" I asked.

"What do you mean?" she said.

"Well, do I put my stuff here and we leave tonight and go someplace else tomorrow? Or how does this work?"

"No, we're here on set," she said. "This is your room for the next five months. Here's the key. Put up pictures. Bring in your music. Do whatever you want."

Even cooler still: The other kids I'm working with, Madison and Olivia and Ethan Wacker, and everyone on the show, are all amazing people. Every day on the set, I learn so much from them. My mom cried when I brought her to the set. She saw my name on my dressing room, looked around, and said, "Holy moly, how did this happen?" Today, I'm still thinking about it. I have two more scenes to shoot this afternoon before I can go home. This weekend, I will be at the Radio Disney Music Awards. And what's really freaky is when I stop to look at what's next, my schedule is completely full through June, when the show premieres.

How did this happen?

It started with a video camera, my brother, and the Internet.

The rest is bizaardvark.

"

I LOVE YOU.

"

THE MYSTERY OF MY
SHAVED EYEBROWS—SOLVED!

Earlier in this book, my mom remembered that I had a mishap with my eyebrows when I was in fourth grade. I have yet to a) admit that it happened or b) explain why I did it. Well, please consider this a confession that there was an accident with a razor. As for why I did it, I saw a picture of a rapper who put three little lines in his eyebrows. I thought it was cool. I decided to put lines in my brows. I got my brother's razor, stood in front of the bathroom mirror, and made the first tiny cut. Except it wasn't as small or precise as I'd intended. It was what I'd call "a little botched."

Then I had to fix the other eyebrow. I wanted them to match. But I botched that one, too. It was hard to get them even. When I finally managed the appropriate symmetry, they were . . . They weren't halved, the way my mom remembers them. Let's just say they were smaller.

Okay?

The mystery of my missing eyebrows is now solved.

P.S. As you can see, they've grown back.

JUST THE GOOD PARTS

When people say, "It's all good," it usually isn't. And the truth is, it's not all good. But there is lots of stuff that is good, and here's the good stuff—at least some of it—according to me.[27]

- Mornings
- The jelly inside a donut
- Friends
- No traffic
- Shorts in the winter
- An empty seat next to you on an airplane
- Letting someone else go first
- Accomplishing a goal
- Driving fast
- Mac and cheese
- Italian food
- Going to the movies
- Getting a text that says, "I like you, too."
- A first kiss

---

27 DM me a list of the stuff you think is good.

- When a friend shares a song you haven't heard before and it's great
- A good workout
- Feeling strong
- Finding one more French fry when you thought the bag was empty
- Getting better at something
- Feeling confident
- That favorite smoothie
- Jumping into the pool
- A cold glass of water on a hot day
- Old photos that make you smile
- Sundays
- You

I AM SO HUNGRY

FOR TODAY.

WHO WANTS TO JOIN ME

FOR A BITE?

THE WORKOUT

Feeling good. Feeling strong. Feeling energized. Feeling like you've done good for yourself. That's the point of going to the gym. Not getting thin, not trying to change yourself, but instead trying to be your best self. I don't smoke or drink. I try to eat healthy foods. And I work out. I go to the gym almost every day. I like the workout, the burn. I like girls who like the gym. What do you do once you're at the gym? What should you do? Lots of people go to the gym and do only one or two things, maybe the treadmill and one of the weight machines, ignoring the rest of the equipment. I've found it's a much better experience if you know what you're doing, if you have a plan. I follow a routine that's evolved over the years. I started working out for football and wrestling, then continued because it made me feel good, and more recently I added a personal trainer to help maximize the time I spend in the gym, because my days are so scheduled. Since I'm frequently asked about my routine, I'm sharing it here. My advice to you is to find someone at your gym, either a pro or someone who knows what they're doing, and ask for help. Most people are happy to give it. And if not, well, that's not a routine you want to follow anyway. So, let's get on with the workout:

Monday (Chest)
- Start out with a 2-mile warm-up
- Bench press (low weights) 3 sets of 10 reps

- Bench press (heavier weight) 3 × 5
- Chest flys 3 × 12
- 100 push-ups
- Dumbbell alternating bench 2 × 8
- Burpees 3 × 10
- 10-minute ab workout (Goal is to get the abs burning. If you don't feel it, flex your abs!)

Tuesday (Back and Biceps)

- 2-mile warm-up jog
- 60 pull-ups in 5 sets
- Bent-over row 3 × 10
- Hammerhead curls 3 × 10
- One-arm row 3 × 10
- Dead lift 3 × 15
- Straight bar curls 3 × 15
- 10-minute ab workout

Wednesday

- Rest day

Thursday (Legs)

- 1-mile warm-up jog
- Stretch your legs really good
- Squats 3 × 10
- Lunges 3 × 12
- One-leg step-ups 3 × 15
- Leg extensions 3 × 10
- High jumps 3 × 15

- Calf raises 3 × 25
- 10-minute ab workout

Friday (Shoulders and Cardio)
- 2-mile sprint intervals
- Shoulder press 3 × 10
- Mountain climbers 3 × 40
- Burpees 3 × 10
- Handstands 3 × failure
- Jump rope 3 minutes × 3
- Shoulder extensions 3 × 8
- 15 minutes of boxing
- 10-minute ab workout

Saturday
- Play a basketball game

Sunday
- Rest day

UPDATES

Team 10: I now have seven people signed: Alissa, Lucas and Marcus, Neels, Alex Lange, A.J. Mitchell, and Tessa Brooks. We're moving into a house soon. We're a reality show waiting to happen. The only goal is to make the best content for fans. You should be following all these people. They're incredible. The future of entertainment is happening right now and it's only going to grow.

Airplane Mode: We found investors and started filming at the end of April 2016. It was crazy to see something that we worked on for nearly two years starting in our apartment, where we wrote and talked about the scenes, get shot. It was surreal. And all of our friends are in it: Jérôme Jarre, Arielle Vandenberg, Anwar Jibawi, Casey Neistat, Amanda Cerny, Roman Atwood, Jerry Purpdrank, Vitaly Zdorovetskiy, Brittany Furlan, and others. The movie should be coming out in late 2016.

Alissa Violet: She's even hotter now.

Logan Paul: He's the lead in *Airplane Mode*, obviously, and killing the acting game. I expect him to keep knocking down movies. My prediction: He becomes the world's biggest action star.

My dad: He bought a boat, and every day he's even more of a legend.

My mom: She's still playing tennis and calling me every day in between sets, making sure I'm alive. "Hey, Mom, so far so good."

Bizaardvark: Since I finished the chapter on the show, we shot nearly the entire first season. It's even better than I thought. Can't wait for you all to see it.

Last Friday: I drove around L.A., pranking people. I made great content.

Yesterday: I did the red carpet at the Radio Disney Music Awards—my way, of course. Instead of walking it, I rode a pink bicycle down it. I also pranked celebrities there. Like I went up to Flo Rida and I said to him, "Hey, Florida, how's it going?" He said, "It's Flo Rida." I dunked a basketball over a bunch of unsuspecting stars. You know, the usual. After, I hung out with Fifth Harmony, Sabrina Carpenter, and Sofia Carson. I skipped the after-after-party and went home and edited videos all night.

Today: Right now, this minute, I'm sitting outside at a restaurant near my house, eating a salad and drinking an incredible chocolate–peanut butter smoothie. It's a beautiful Sunday afternoon here in Hollywood.

Tomorrow: I will be on the set of *Bizaardvark* at 9 a.m. and working on various projects. By now, you know this about me: It's not living the dream. It's building the dream.

EPILOGUE—5 TIPS FOR GETTING MORE FOLLOWERS

I think a lot of people my age and younger think it would be cool to be Vine famous or Instagram famous—famous, in general, on social media. It's like when my parents were younger, and they and their friends fantasized about becoming rock stars. The next generation wanted to be rappers. Now, you and me, we're all about social media and having lots of likes and followers. Which is really our desire, like anyone, to be liked by a lot of people, friends. Don't ya think? Anyway, people constantly ask me how they can get more followers. If you're one of those people, or even if you aren't but are interested enough to have made it this far in the book, I'm going to tell you how to up your social-media game. I've boiled it down to five main tips. They've worked for me—but as you'll likely see, they apply to more than just the Internet.

1. Consistency

Post content every day. The more you post, the better you'll get at posting, and you will also grow your followers. As you grow followers, they'll look for content from you. Consistency. Reliability. Those are keys to becoming a good habit in someone's life. You want people to look for your content in their feed the way they look around for a friend. Be as unpredictable and entertaining as your imagination allows with your content, but be that consistent friend other people can count on.

2. Find a Niche

Post stuff that is different from what other people post. This gives people a reason to follow you. People don't want to follow two of the same people. In other words, be unique. Find that thing about you and what you like that makes you different from everyone else in the world; then celebrate it, share it, do it all with the authenticity that comes from being real, and then watch it blow up.

3. Collab

Always find people to make content with. This is a great way to grow each other's audiences. Even if you have five hundred followers, collaborations are beneficial. The best part of collabs, though, is getting to work with other people. You help each other. Also, and this is really true: The best way to find yourself, to discover what you're all about, whether it's your sense of humor or your sense of self, is through other people.

4. Videos

Everyone wants to just post pictures and be cute. NO, don't do it. Resist the urge. Instead, make videos. Videos are key. Videos show your personality, and people will learn to love you quicker. They want to see the different parts of you. I know it's a risk to reveal so much of yourself, but it's worth it.

5. Be Yourself

People can tell when you're being yourself, and they're attracted to that. No one wants to follow the person that is clearly trying to be cool and act like they're awesome. . . . I SEE THROUGH THAT BS. Online and off, the most awesome person you can possibly be is yourself. That's what this book is all about. Being yourself, being authentic, pursuing whatever that thing is that you love, that thing that makes you the best you, and not worrying about what anyone else thinks, and then going for it. I mean, GOING FOR IT! Because you can do and be it all, everything you want and dream.

YOU GOTTA WANT IT!

ACKNOWLEDGMENTS

The only thing better than hearing "thank you" is saying it—and I have a ton of people to thank for everything, starting with my brother, Logan. Thanks for keeping me motivated and working as hard as me to push each other. We are on a crazy journey, and it's just the start, bro. #RiseOfThePauls

Thank you to the fans. Without you guys, none of this is possible. Your support is amazing, and we've truly become best friends these past couple of months. This is just the start. We are a family. Let's keep it close. Love you to death. <3

Thank you to everyone on Team 10 for believing in my vision. If you're reading this, you know the mountains we've climbed and the challenges we've faced, and it's all paying off. No one will ever know those behind-the-scenes things. Well, maybe—if one day we turn it all into a reality show. Love you guys for real.

Neels: You will be the biggest DJ.

A.J.: Can't wait to see your singing career be massive.

Alissa: You are the coolest girl I know. I'll see you on the runway!

Lucas and Marcus: To this day, your dancing blows me away. Oh, and no one can make me laugh as hard as you guys can.

Alex: How are you fifteen? WTF? I can't wait to see what you have going on when you're my age. Girls will die. You are the homie and are going to be a teen sensation.

Tessa: The only word I can use to describe you is DOPE. Everything you do is DOPE. You're going to kill it!!

To anyone who has joined Team 10 since writing this . . . you should've joined sooner . . . lol jk ily . . .

Thank you to Alex Shekarchian for hustling for me every day. You've opened up awesome doors for me. You're the man and ahead of your time! YOU GET IT!

Thank you to Krazy Remi for teaching me to be a boss. That's all I gotta say! DREWWW WOO WOOOOO!

Thank you to the Disney family. From the cast and crew of *Bizaardvark* to the casting and execs, you guys have changed my life. I am forever grateful. You all believed in me and saw how important digital is. THANK YOU!

DeVore: Alex? lol!

Ethan: I beat you in H.O.R.S.E (it's even more official now).

Olivia: Please sing more on Instagram. I die.

Madison: What's your favorite show? *Bizaardvark*. What's your . . . *BIZAARDVARK*.

Thank you to my lawyer, Phil Daniels. I am on the phone with you more than anyone. You're hands down the best lawyer for social and traditional talent—and of course me. Thanks for believing in me!

Thank you to my high-school wrestling coaches. When I was getting big on social media, you guys were the only ones left who still supported me and pushed me every day! I wish I could've wrestled my senior year! I would've won State! ;)

Ant: Duger down!!!!!!!

Percival: Bang Bang! Sosa!

Deluca: If you still want to be Christian Bale, I have the connects now!! lol!

Jed: Thanks for being in my corner when these other guys were with Logan! lol!

Thank you to some of my business advisors: Cory Levy, Mike Giuliano, Alex Debelov, Spencer Hopkins, Patrick Bush, Paolo Moreno, and Cat Schwartz.

Thank you to everyone involved in *Airplane Mode*. It was such a journey that paid off.

Thank you to the employees at Team 10 for working long hours and odd jobs. We will rise!

Thank you to Drake for keeping that fire going. There isn't anyone making good songs anymore. I try to relate what I do on social and in business to your career. You'll call me one day, and when you do . . . we gon do something great.

Todd Gold: Thank you for helping me tell this crazy story and doing it so good . . . and at least acting like you were entertained by it. ;)

Dan Strone: Thank you for holding my hand through this process and making it super simple. I learned a lot from you, and you're a savage.

Chelsea Grogan: Thank you for dealing with all the photos for the book and the craziness that went along with that! You're the bomb!

Thank you to everyone at Simon & Schuster: Carolyn Reidy, Louise Burke, Jen Bergstrom, Nina Cordes, Stephanie DeLuca, and John Vairo. Also a special thanks to my editor, Jeremie Ruby-Strauss, for being ahead of trends, talent, and bestsellers—and spotting me.

John Ferriter and Jamie Gruttemeyer: Thank you for putting this deal together and making it happen. You guys have believed in me from the start of my traditional media career, and for that I'm forever grateful.

And finally, thank you, thank you, and thank you to my mom and dad: Thank you for the continuous support and allowing me to live my dreams. You guys are instrumental to the way I live my life every day. This is just the start!

PHOTO CREDITS

Text

page 14: Photograph by Neels Visser, @neelsvisser

pages 106, 195 and 207: Courtesy of the author

Insert

page 1: Photograph by Max Goodrich

page 2:
top left: Photograph by Raymond Cheng/Best Image Photography
top right: Courtesy of Proud Pops of Jake!
bottom left: Courtesy of Pam Stepnick
bottom right: Courtesy of Proud Pops of Jake!

pages 3, 4, 5, 6, and 7: Photographs by Max Goodrich

page 8: Photograph by Alissa Violet